ASSURING CHILD SUPPORT

ASSURING CHILD SUPPORT

An Extension of Social Security

Irwin Garfinkel

RUSSELL SAGE FOUNDATION / NEW YORK

The Russell Sage Foundation

The Russell Sage Foundation, one of the oldest of America's general purpose foundations, was established in 1907 by Mrs. Margaret Olivia Sage for "the improvement of social and living conditions in the United States." The Foundation seeks to fulfill this mandate by fostering the development and dissemination of knowledge about the political, social, and economic problems of America.

The Board of Trustees is responsible for oversight and the general policies of the Foundation, while administrative direction of the program and staff is vested in the President, assisted by the officers and staff. The President bears final responsibility for the decision to publish a manuscript as a Russell Sage Foundation book. In reaching a judgment on the competence, accuracy, and objectivity of each study, the President is advised by the staff and selected expert readers. The conclusions and interpretations in Russell Sage Foundation publications are those of the authors and not of the Foundation, its Trustees, or its staff. Publication by the Foundation, therefore, does not imply endorsement of the contents of the study.

Library of Congress Cataloging-in-Publication Data

Garfinkel, Irwin.
    Assuring child support / Irwin Garfinkel.
        p.   cm.
    Includes bibliographical references and index.
    ISBN 0-87154-300-1
    1. Child support—United States.   2. Child support—Economic aspects.
    I. Title.
    HV742.G38   1992   92-15042
    362.7'1—dc20   CIP

The paper used in this publication meets the minimum requirements of American National Standard for Information Sciences—Permanence of Paper for Printed Library Materials, ANSI Z39.48-1984.

RUSSELL SAGE FOUNDATION
112 East 64th Street, New York, New York 10021

10   9   8   7   6   5   4   3   2   1

Contents

Preface and Acknowledgments

In the late 1960s and early 1970s, I, like many other liberals, thought of child support enforcement principally as a method of harassing welfare mothers. The fathers of poor children on welfare were themselves poor, so, as the saying goes, "You can't get blood from a stone." Conservatives had their own reasons for opposing child support enforcement. In general, conservatives support the status quo. Also, some subscribe to the view that after all, "Boys will be boys." My beliefs about child support enforcement were part of a much broader consensus that, in this area, government should "let well enough alone." My beliefs and that consensus have since shifted dramatically.

In 1974, Congress narrowly passed the Child Support Enforcement Amendments to the Social Security Act, which created the federal Office of Child Support Enforcement. Senator Russell Long of Louisiana was the principal sponsor of the act. In response to this change in government policy, the Assistant Secretary for Planning and Evaluation in the federal department of Health, Education, and Welfare requested the Institute for Research on Poverty (IRP) at the University of Wisconsin to conduct some research on child support. I was then the director designate of the IRP. Fortunately, I was able to locate a graduate student in social work who was both very capable and very interested in writing a dissertation on child support enforcement. Supervising Judith Cassetty's dissertation, which was subsequently published as a book entitled *The Child Support Obligation*, led me to change my mind.

Since 1977 I have studied, written about, and had some influence on our child support system. This book summarizes what I have learned. It reflects my background as a social worker and an economist. I studied economics in order to do better social work. Social workers are charged by society with helping the disadvantaged lead more rewarding lives. That we must serve two masters, the disadvantaged and society at large, sometimes makes our work difficult. Economists are taught to search for efficient solutions, those in which the benefits exceed the costs. I changed my mind about child support enforcement because research convinced me that government assurance of child support could simultaneously reduce economic insecurity and welfare dependence at little or no extra cost to the government. As a social worker, it is my responsibility to advocate a change that might benefit not only the poor but also the greater society. As a social scientist, it is my responsibility to present a balanced analysis of the benefits and costs of alternatives. I have tried to fulfill both responsibilities in this book.

There is another way in which the book reflects the idiosyncracies of my background. My parents were communists. Unlike most American children, who are told that socialism is bad, I was told that capitalism is bad. The closest thing to adolescent rebellion against authority that I undertook was to argue with my parents about the relative merits of socialism and capitalism. Despite our disagreements, which at times got heated, they loved and respected me, and I certainly loved and respected them. These teenage debates about the appropriate role of the individual and the government kindled a lifelong interest in the topic. This book deals with one very interesting aspect of this topic: the appropriate role of government in assuring economic support for children who live apart from one of their parents. The heated teenage debates also prepared me to disregard labels and find common ground with those from all sides of the political spectrum. Over the years, I discovered—at first with dismay and then, increasingly, with delight—that I could not predict someone's position on child support assurance by whether he or she was a Republican or a Democrat, a liberal or a conservative.

Finally, my work on child support and this book also reflect my long tenure at IRP at the University of Wisconsin. The Institute was created by the Office of Economic Opportunity (OEO) in 1966 to be the "think tank" for the War on Poverty. That the think tank was located at the University of Wisconsin was no accident. At the beginning of the twentieth century, Wisconsin, under the leadership of Governor (and subsequently Senator) Lafollette, established the nation's first social insurance program, workmen's compensation. John R. Commons, a professor of economics at the University of Wisconsin had designed the program. His students were responsible one generation later, in 1932, for creating the nation's first unemployment insurance system. One of them, Edwin Witte, was appointed by President Franklin D. Roosevelt to become the Executive Secretary of the Committee on Economic Security. During his six months' leave of absence from the university, Witte directed the committee in the design of the landmark 1935 Social Security Act, which created old-age and unemployment insurance, as well as the aid to families with dependent children program.

A generation later, in 1963, one of Witte's students, Robert Lampman, while on leave from his job as a professor of economics at the University of Wisconsin to serve as a staff member of President Kennedy's Council of Economic Advisors, was a principal author of the chapter on poverty in the 1963 Economic Report of the President. Burton Weisbrod, co-author of the poverty chapter, joined Lampman at Wisconsin when he left the Council of Economic Advisors. Thus, when OEO decided to create a think tank, locating it at the University of Wisconsin was a natural thing to do because a good chunk of the nation's economics expertise on the matter was there.

Over the years, Professor Lampman convinced me of the importance of economic insecurity, filled my ears with stories about Witte and Commons, and convinced me of their wisdom. I learned that Lafollette had been the conservative, Madison candidate for governor. The genius of Commons and Witte was to inject selective doses of socialism into a predominantly capitalist system in such a way as to increase economic security while reinforcing productivity, efficiency, and, ultimately, capitalism itself. Their most successful tool was social insurance. The child support assurance proposal that I advocate is a clear descendant of the Commons-Witte-Lampman approach to reducing economic insecurity.

So many people help any professor who writes a book. I have been especially lucky. My colleagues at the IRP stimulated and encouraged me for twenty years. Robert Lampman has been a great teacher and a kind father figure. The book is dedicated to him and to the Institute for Research on Poverty. Sara McLanahan has been my closest intellectual collaborator since the early 1980s. Without her, this book would probably not be. Marygold Melli, Phillip Robins, David Betson, Sandra Danziger, Maurice Macdonald, Mette Sorenson, Nora Schaeffer, and Judith Seltzer have also been co-investigators and co-authors in the child support project, as well as good friends. Robert Haveman, my predecessor as IRP director, has been a good friend and colleague for twenty years, set a good example by writing books, and informed me that it was about time that I wrote a book about child support. Harold Watts, the first director of the IRP, not only hired and encouraged me, but also gave me the idea of using the income tax mechanism to enforce child support. Judith Cassetty was the first of a wonderful group of students who wrote dissertations or published research on child support. Through their research on child support, Cassetty and Professors Ann Nichols Casebolt, Thomas Corbett, Marieka Klawitter, Donald Oellerich, Dan Meyer, James Moran, and Patrick Wong have educated the nation in general and me in particular. Working with them has also been a source of great pleasure for me. The project managers for the state contract, Ann Nichols Casebolt, Anne Lewis, and Pat Brown, made my life more manageable and enjoyable. Over the years, John Flescher and Louisa Cunliffe provided programming assistance. Elizabeth Phillips, Yeun Hee Kim, Kwi Ryung, Jared Bernstein, and John Robertson supplied research assistance.

My work in child support has also been influenced by many researchers from other institutions. Four stand out: Barbara Bergmann and Isabel Sawhill, for their pioneering work on women and child support, and Alfred Kahn and Sheila Kamerman, for their pioneering work on cross-national social welfare policy.

I also owe an enormous debt of gratitude to my colleagues in government. Collectively, they turned an academic vision into a practical reality. Sherwood Zink, counsel for the Wisconsin office of child support enforcement, educated me about child support law and was responsible for forging and maintaining the state–university link. Ada Skyles and Ingrid Rothe spent hours hammering out the details of reform and bridging the gap between research and policy. Severa Austin provided a dose of energy and commitment at a crucial time. Donald Percy, Secretary of the Wisconsin Department of Health and Social Services from 1978 to 1982, was the first administrator to take seriously the proposal for a new child support assurance system. John Palmer, Assistant Secretary of Planning and Evaluation in the federal Department of Health and Human Services, and Barbara Torrey, director of research, hired me for the fall semester in 1980 to work for the department designing and estimating the costs and benefits of the new system. The early support of these three administrators was critical. I am also indebted to the secretaries who followed Percy and continued to contract with me and the IRP to evaluate the state's child support system: Linda Reivitz, Timothy Cullen, Patricia Goodrich, and Gerald Whitburn. Most important, Tom Loftus, Speaker of the Wisconsin Assembly from 1982 to 1990, as a freshman legislator and member of the Wisconsin Welfare Reform Committee appointed by Secretary Percy, became an increasingly influential advocate of child support assurance and, ultimately, shepherded through the legislation that took Wisconsin toward a child support assurance system.

Most of the funding for my research came from a series of grants from the Ford Foundation program in urban poverty. I don't know what I would have done without the support of the program's officers in the foundation's urban poverty program: Prudence Brown, Shelby Miller, Gordon Berlin, and John Lanigan, especially Prue. Eric Wanner, President of the Russell Sage Foundation, invited me to be a visiting scholar to begin writing this book in 1989, provided additional research support, and, most important, invested his own editorial skills and hired Marin Gazzaniga to help me reshape the book and make it more accessible. The Foundation for Child Development and Barbara Blum have also provided more recent funding and personal encouragement. Liz Uhr edited early drafts of this manuscript and helped me create order out of chaos. Gazzaniga made it more like a silk purse than a sow's ear.

Finally, our children, Sara, Jay, Leah, Anna, and Lynn, helped me to sharpen some arguments and, together with my wife, Sara, remained throughout the most important source of encouragement.

1 / Introduction

TOO MANY POOR AND INSECURE AMERICAN CHILDREN

Today, about one of five children in the United States is officially defined as poor. And official definitions of poverty are not gener ous. In 1991, to be classified by the federal government as poor, a family with three persons had to have an annual income below $11,140; a family with four persons, below $13,400. Moreover, the proportion of poor children increased from 15 percent in 1974 to 20 percent in 1989.[1] Poverty among children is on the rise.

Poverty is but one form of economic insecurity that affects the nation's youth. A much larger proportion, perhaps up to one-half, of American children are likely to experience severe episodes of economic insecurity. For example, about one-half of all children who live in families headed by single mothers are poor.[2] But even among nonpoor families headed by mothers, the average drop in income after divorce or separation is 50 percent.[3] And many two-parent families within the bottom half of the income dis-tribution commonly experience periodic descents into poverty.[4] None of America's major economic competitors—Germany, Japan, Canada, Great Britain, France, Denmark, Norway, or Sweden—

allows such a large proportion of its children to suffer such relative deprivation.[5]

Are poverty and insecurity really harmful to children? Do they really threaten America's future competitiveness as a nation? After all, some children who grow up in difficult economic circumstances do well, sometimes exceedingly well, and there may even be some who are ennobled by the experience. But social science tells us that these cases represent the exception, rather than the rule. On average, children who grow up in poverty are more likely to drop out of school than children who grow up in more affluent circumstances, to conceive children out of wedlock, and to become poor and dependent on welfare as adults.[6]

Some analysts dismiss such findings by correctly noting that correlation does not prove causation. It may not be poverty or insecurity that breeds poverty, they argue, but rather, for example, heredity. If the parents are poor, that can reflect lack of innate ability, which they pass on directly to their children. In the absence of an experiment in which we randomly assign children to poverty, insecurity, and affluence, it is impossible to completely rule out the possibility that poverty is hereditary in that sense. But at least one experiment of just this sort has been conducted with animals, and the results are quite informative.

Leonard Rosenblum conducted a series of experiments that investigated the effects of poverty and insecurity on the well-being of young monkeys. It is difficult not to think about his findings in human terms. In one experiment, he randomly assigned three groups of monkey mothers and their infants to three different feeding environments. In each group the monkeys had to extract food that was hidden in their pens. The researchers provided all three groups with enough food to sustain normal adult weights and infant growth. One group had to make very little effort to find the food. The second group had to work very hard to get their food. The third group alternately faced the easy and the difficult environment.

The results? The mothers in the easy environment developed the calmest, most secure relationships with their infants, and the infants developed the most independence. The mothers in the difficult environment were more prone to cut off interactions with their infants, and the infants exhibited more signs of emotional disturbance and became less independent. The worst group, however, were the ones subjected to the variable feeding environment. The mothers in this group were the most likely of the three groups to cut off interactions with their offspring, and the offspring exhibited the most signs of emotional disturbance including a pattern of behavior that has been labeled *depression*. "The infants for 10–20 minutes at a time, closed their eyes and maintained a hunched posture while clasping their own bodies or while clinging to or leaning against a partner."[7]

These findings dramatically demonstrate the ill effects on monkeys of a poor environment and the even more damaging effects of insecurity. The same environmental effects may or may not hold true for human beings, but it is difficult to see why children should be less sensitive to the effects of stress on their mothers than are young monkeys. Moreover, it is worth noting that what we know about the relationship between cancer and smoking also comes from correlational findings for human beings and experiments with animals. Just as with smoking, the evidence of the adverse consequences of poverty and insecurity, although indirect, is strong enough to warrant energetic countermeasures. Reducing economic insecurity and poverty is not only compassionate but probably also wise.

This book focuses on one method of attacking poverty and economic insecurity among one group of poor children. It is a method I have been involved in developing and testing since the late 1970s. The group of children that this method aims to help are those who spend at least part of their childhood living with only their mothers. (Appendix 1.A provides a more complete description of just who these families are.) The method is government assurance of private child support; the specific plan is called the Child Support Assurance System (CSAS).

SINGLE PARENTHOOD, POVERTY, ECONOMIC SECURITY, AND DEPENDENCE

A large part of the poverty problem, as mentioned, is associated with single parenthood. Nearly half of all poor children live with only their mothers.[8] Moreover, poor children in single-mother families are poorer than poor children in two-parent families—

and they stay poor longer. Even the more fortunate children living in single-mother families that are not poor suffer from the economic insecurity that results from the 50 percent decrease in living standards associated with divorce or separation.[9] Thus, although poverty among children from single-mother homes by no means accounts for all poverty among children, it is both an important and a particularly virulent form of child poverty.

Another important reason to focus efforts to reduce poverty and insecurity on children who live in single-mother families is that this family configuration has been growing rapidly. As of 1987, 16.9 million, or about 27 percent, of American children age eighteen or younger resided apart from at least one of their natural parents.[10] Increases in divorce, separation, and out-of-wedlock births had more than doubled the proportion of children in this circumstance in less than three decades.[11] Demographic projections indicate that over half of the children born in the 1980s will live apart from one parent before they reach adulthood.[12] In other words, over half of the next generation will have spent at least part of their childhood living in families headed by a single mother.

There is a third reason for focusing on children who live with single mothers. Just as about half of the children who live with single mothers are poor, so, too, during the course of a year, about half become dependent upon welfare.[13] That both fractions are about half is not accidental. Poverty leads inexorably to welfare dependence. Conversely, as we shall see later, government's overdependence on welfare as the answer to the problems of single mothers actually contributes to the poverty problem by neglecting prevention and by enticing mothers with low-earning capacity to rely too heavily on welfare.

Although there is debate about whether dependence on welfare is harmful to children (see chapter 2 and footnote 40 therein), it seems fair to imagine that it is not a positive experience. And, even in a so-called generous state like New York, Aid to Families with Dependent Children (AFDC) and food stamp benefits bring a family's income to only 90 percent of the poverty line.[14] Moreover, as the conservative analyst Lawrence Mead pointed out, long-term dependence is inconsistent with equality, for a dependent is not an equal.[15] The rationale behind the Child Support

Assurance System, therefore, is to reduce welfare dependence, as well as poverty and insecurity.

THE NEED FOR CHILD SUPPORT

In *Single Mothers and Their Children: A New American Dilemma,* Sara McLanahan and I examined the problems of mother-only families, the increase in the number of such families between 1940 and 1983, the history of public policy toward single mothers and their children from colonial times through 1980, and the Reagan administration's policy initiatives and their effects on the economic security and independence of single mothers.

McLanahan and I argued that, at every point in the nation's history, the United States has confronted a dilemma of whether to give greater priority to reducing the economic insecurity and poverty of mother-only families or to reducing the number of such families and the degree of their dependence on government. Such families have always been disproportionately represented among the poor, and many children who grow up in these families are clearly disadvantaged. As adults they have lower socioeconomic status; they are more likely to become single parents themselves, through either out-of-wedlock births or divorce; and they are more likely to be dependent on government. As noted, many of these problems are traceable to the economic insecurity and poverty of the families in which they grew up. Government can reduce these economic problems by supplementing the incomes of these families. But doing so may increase their dependence on government and their prevalence.[16]

The argument in this book takes into account both aspects of this dilemma. One of my central objectives here is to examine in detail the extent to which a new Child Support Assurance System could resolve the dilemma by simultaneously increasing the security of mother-only families and reducing their dependence on government.

First, some semantics. Throughout this book, I use the term *nonresident parent* rather than *noncustodial parent* because nonresidence, rather than the absence or presence of legal custody, is what makes an explicit transfer of money for child support necessary. Whether the nonresident parent shares legal custody with the child has no implications for child support, whereas if the nonresident parent shares residence with the child regularly, that is becomes the resident parent, there are clear implications for child support.[17] As used in this book, the term *child support* refers to an income transfer to a caretaker, usually the mother, of a child with a nonresident parent. If the money comes from the nonresident parent, it is private child support. If the money comes from the government, it is public child support. Because the nonresident parent is so often the father, I shall refer to this parent as *him* throughout the book; to the resident parent, as *she*.

THE RATIONALE BEHIND CHILD SUPPORT

In all societies, support for children comes from both their families and the broader community.[18] The division of this private and public responsibility has differed across and within societies throughout history. Roman law required that parents not only meet the living expenses of their children but also pay for their education.[19] In 1848, when the sixth plank of the Communist Manifesto called for the establishment of free public education, most of the northern United States was already providing free public education through the elementary grades. During the late nineteenth and early twentieth centuries, all Western industrialized countries socialized the costs of elementary and secondary education. Similarly, all but the United States now also provide national health insurance and children's allowances. Still, in advanced industrial societies, except for the poorest part of the population, the principal source of support for children is their natural parents.

Except in the most egregious cases of child neglect and abuse, governments do not supervise or otherwise interfere with the manner in which parents provide for their children. The provision of economic support to a child by a nonresident parent, however, is more problematic. Aside from the practical complications of an explicit transfer of resources from the parent not living in the child's home to the child's adult custodian, there are the personal complications. Parents who are not living together often do not like, or even trust, one another. In some cases the resident parent may not want any contact with the nonresident parent (for example, if a mother is afraid of an abusive former husband). For such reasons, securing economic support from nonresident parents has not been easy. As a result, all Western countries have laws regulating the obligation of nonresident parents to support their children.

WEAKNESSES OF THE U.S. CHILD SUPPORT SYSTEM

Given that more than one-half of the children in the next generation will be potentially eligible for child support, the quality of America's child support institutions should be of vital concern to the nation. And, in fact, the legislative reforms of the child support system since the mid-1970s demonstrate that this is a serious concern. The 1975 Child Support Enforcement Amendments took the first steps toward substantial reform of our child support system—and toward adoption of the CSAS.

Prior to 1975, child support was nearly exclusively a state and local matter. State laws established the duty of nonresident parents to pay child support but left all the details up to local courts.[20] Judges had the authority to decide whether any child support should be paid and, if so, how much. They also had full authority over what action would be taken if nonresident parents failed to pay, jail being the most severe punishment.

In 1979, the U.S. Census Bureau began gathering data on child support every other year. The first census study indicated that nearly two-thirds of nonresident parents paid no child support.[21] The details of the study revealed weaknesses at every step in the child support process. Only six of ten mothers potentially eligible for child support had child support awards. Among those with legal awards, about half received the full amount to which they were entitled, and over a quarter received nothing. Few people argued with the conclusion that the system condoned parental irresponsibility.

Other studies documented alleged inequities in child support enforcement. Child support awards for children and parents in similar economic circumstances varied widely.[22] Whereas most nonresident fathers paid no child support and suffered no consequences, thousands of others were sent to jail.[23] And poor nonresident fathers who were legally obligated to pay child support were required to pay a substantially higher proportion of their incomes than middle- and, especially, upper-income nonresident fathers.[24] Finally, nearly half the single mothers and their children were poor and dependent on welfare.[25]

This last fact underlies what is perhaps the most serious criticism of the public child support system, which consists principally of the AFDC program and related welfare programs such as Medicaid and Food Stamps: that it fails to prevent poverty while encouraging dependency. Two-thirds of the current beneficiaries of AFDC will be dependent on welfare for eight or more years.[26] Can poverty among children living with single mothers be prevented, rather than just alleviated? Can poor, single mothers be helped in ways that promote their independence?

A NEW CHILD SUPPORT ASSURANCE SYSTEM

Growing awareness of, and research into, the weaknesses of the child support system have spawned innumerable proposals for reform and a flurry of legislation at both the state and federal levels. The CSAS is noteworthy in its simplicity, its encapsulation of existing trends, and its influence on actual legislation. The plan is this: All parents living apart from their children would be obligated to share income with them. The sharing rate, or percentage of the nonresident parent's income to be shared, would be specified by law and would depend only upon the number of children owed support. The resulting child support obligation would be collected through payroll withholding, as are income taxes and social security taxes. A child with a living, nonresident parent would be entitled to benefits equal to either the child support paid by the nonresident parent or a socially assured minimum benefit, whichever was higher. Should the nonresident parent pay less than the assured benefit, the government would make up the difference.

As I will detail in the next chapter, in recent years, the United States Congress has enacted several major pieces of legislation that entice or require the states to make major changes in their private child support enforcement systems to make them more like the collection features of the CSAS.

Do these changes make sense? How effective have they been?

What are their benefits and costs? Should the nation go even further and adopt a full-fledged child support assurance system? What are the benefits and costs of an assured child support benefit? These are the questions this book will explore.

RESPONSIBILITY FOR SUPPORTING CHILDREN:
A PHILOSOPHICAL, IDEOLOGICAL, AND PRACTICAL ISSUE

Why should government require natural parents to support their children? There is the obvious argument that the natural parents' responsibility to their children is a moral imperative.[27] In addition, there is a more utilitarian argument for public enforcement of private child support: to minimize the public costs of providing support. Protecting the public purse justifies much greater government enforcement of private child support than most people think. During the course of a year, nearly half of the families headed by single mothers receive welfare. Moreover, there is little doubt that the proportion needing welfare at any time would increase quite dramatically in the absence of any public enforcement of private child support.[28]

Why should government support children who are needy? Once again, in addition to the moral correctness of such a policy, there are utilitarian arguments. Increasing the security of poor children is an investment in the future labor force. It promotes domestic tranquility. Finally, the existence of a social safety net facilitates the working of capitalism. Capitalism is dynamic because businesses are allowed to fail. A strong safety net is far more efficient than protecting jobs and businesses from extinction. That is why British and American governments have assumed responsibility for supporting their destitute citizens, including children, at least since the enactment of the Elizabethan Poor Laws of 1601.[29] Indeed, Adam Smith, the apostle of laissez faire, accepted the principle of public responsibility for the poor.[30] He also criticized the immobility of labor, which arose out of local financing and administration of the poor law.

The libertarian Right finds these justifications wanting. They do not grant the premise that the state should provide for its destitute citizens. The libertarian Right also attacks public enforcement of private child support obligations because of a belief that government should not be in the business of coercing citizens to do things they would not do voluntarily. To paraphrase George Gilder, government should not be in the business of taming unwilling, wild men.[31]

At the other extreme, the Far Left resists public enforcement of private child support because to advocate child support enforcement is to admit that the costs of childrearing should not be completely socialized. As noted, some of these costs have already been socialized through free public education in the United States and through child allowances elsewhere. Public enforcement of private child support obligations is incompatible with complete socialization of the costs of childrearing, an ideal that appeals to the Left because it is the most egalitarian policy. Leftist critics of public enforcement also note that, in the current context, the increasing of child support payments has the effect of transferring income from poor fathers of children currently on welfare to middle-income families, via reductions in their taxes. The liberal critics are right about this. But, as I will show after weighing the costs and benefits of the CSAS, that does not justify abandoning government enforcement of child support. (Whether poor nonresident fathers should be required to pay child support is discussed in greater detail in Chapter 7.) To further complicate matters, the Left is now split on child support enforcement because, whereas enforcement redistributes regressively across class lines, within classes it redistributes from men to women.

Most people are not too concerned with these ideological arguments of the Far Right and the Far Left. The general public's approach to child support assurance is less ideological and more practical: Will child support guidelines and routine income withholding increase child support payments? Will an assured benefit increase taxes? By how much? Although philosophy and ideology are not entirely ignored, this book focuses on answering these kinds of practical questions.

ORGANIZATION OF THE BOOK

The book is organized around the contrast between the traditional child support system and a newly emerging child support assurance system. Chapter 2 reviews the history of the U.S. government's policies toward poor single mothers and describes the structures and analyzes the shortcomings of the private and public child support system. Chapter 3 describes the new child support assurance system toward which the nation is evolving and discusses some of the benefits and costs of the new system. Chapter 4 explores the question of how much more child support can be collected. The fifth chapter compares and contrasts the two most widely adopted guidelines for determining the size of child support awards. The sixth chapter considers the case for an assured child support benefit and explores the benefits and costs of alternative kinds of assured benefits. Chapter 7 addresses the most common criticisms of the CSAS. The final chapter summarizes the case for complete adoption of a child support assurance system as an effective way to combat economic insecurity and welfare dependence for future generations.

APPENDIX 1.A/FAMILIES OF CHILDREN POTENTIALLY ELIGIBLE FOR CHILD SUPPORT

When most people think about children who could be eligible for child support, they assume that these children live in families headed by single mothers. Nearly two-thirds do fit the stereotype. But 15 percent of families with children eligible for support are headed by single fathers, and in another 21 percent the mother is remarried.[32]

Who are the single mothers who make up the majority of those potentially eligible for child support? This appendix provides a more detailed picture of resident mothers—and nonresident fathers.

More than one-third of mothers of children potentially eligible for child support are divorced or remarried, about one-seventh are separated, and about two-ninths have never been married. The bulk of the mothers living apart from fathers are white. Yet, about a quarter are black, and nearly another 10 percent are Hispanic. In view of the higher rates of divorce and out-of-wedlock births among blacks and Hispanics, their disproportionate representation is not surprising.[33]

The mothers are not highly educated. One-quarter of them have not completed high school. Nearly another half have completed high school but have received no further education. Less than 10 percent have completed college.

Because lack of education often translates into low earning power, it is not surprising that a large proportion of the families—nearly one-third—live in poverty. The economic status of the mothers and children is strongly related to the mother's marital status. Less than one in ten remarried mothers is poor. In stark contrast, well over one-half of the families of the never-married mothers are poor. Finally, only 5 percent of these women have four or more children. Another 10 percent have three children. One-third have two children, and over half have only one child.

Because there are no good national surveys of nonresident fathers, the picture of them is a bit more sketchy than the picture of resident mothers.[34] Yet it is possible to piece together a decent picture of nonresident fathers by considering the mirror image of resident mothers. Demographers tell us that like tends to mate with like.[35] On the basis of knowledge about resident mothers, therefore, it can be inferred that the bulk of nonresident fathers are white, about a quarter are black, and nearly another 10 percent are Hispanic. Similarly, it can be assumed that, like the mothers, about one-quarter of the fathers have not completed high school, nearly another half have completed high school but have no additional education, and less than 10 percent have completed college.

Because for each divorced and separated mother there is a divorced and separated father, the percentages are the same: More than one-third of the nonresident fathers must be divorced or remarried and about one-seventh must be separated. Furthermore, because divorced men are more likely to remarry than divorced women, and 43 percent of the divorced mothers are remarried, it can be assumed that more than 43 percent of the nonresident fathers are remarried. Similarly, less than two-ninths of the fathers have never married.

NOTES

1. U.S. House of Representatives, Committee on Ways and Means, *Overview of Entitlement Programs: 1991 Green Book*, Washington D.C.: U.S. Government Printing Office, 1991, Table 64, p. 1051.

2. Irwin Garfinkel and Sara S. McLanahan, *Single Mothers and Their Children: A New American Dilemma*, Washington, D.C.: Urban Institute Press, 1986, p. 12.

3. Greg J. Duncan and Saul D. Hoffman, "A Reconsideration of the Economic Consequences of Marital Dissolution," *Demography*, Vol. 22, No. 4, 1985, pp. 485–497.

4. See Greg J. Duncan, Richard D. Coe, Mary E. Corcoran, Martha S. Hill, Saul D. Hoffman, and James N. Morgan, *Years of Poverty, Years of Plenty: The Changing Economic Fortunes of American Workers and Families*, Ann Arbor, Mich.: The University of Michigan, Institute for Social Research, 1984. See also Mary J. Bane and David T. Ellwood, "Slipping into and out of Poverty: The Dynamics of Spells," *Journal of Human Resources*, Vol. 21, No. 1, 1986, pp. 1–23.

5. Sheldon Danziger and Jonathan Stern, "The Causes and Consequences of Child Poverty in the United States," in *Child Poverty in Industrialized Countries*, special subseries, Unicef Economic Policies Series 10, Florence, Italy: International Child Development Centre, November 1990.

6. Sara S. McLanahan, "The Reproduction of Poverty," *American Journal of Sociology*, Vol. 90, 1985, pp. 873–901; Gary D. Sandefur, Sara S. McLanahan, and R. A. Wojtkiewicz, "Race and Ethnicity, Family Structure and High School Graduation," Discussion Paper #893–89, Madison, Wis.: Institute for Research on Poverty, University of Wisconsin-Madison, 1989; S. F. Krein and A. H. Beller, "Educational Attainment of Children from Single-Parent Families: Differences by Exposure, Gender, and Race," *Demography*, Vol. 25, 1988, pp. 221–224; Nan M. Astone and Sara S. McLanahan, "The Effect of Family Structure on School Completion," paper presented at the annual meetings of the Population Association of America, Baltimore, March 1989; Sara S. McLanahan, "Family Structure and Dependency: Early Transitions to Female Household Headship," *Demography*, Vol. 25, 1988, pp. 1–16.

7. Leonard Rosenblum and Gayle S. Paully, "The Effects of Varying Environmental Demands on Maternal and Infant Behavior," *Child Development*, Vol. 55, 1984, pp. 305–314.

8. Garfinkel and McLanahan, *Single Mothers*, p. 12.

9. Duncan and Hoffman, "Marital Dissolution." Thirty-eight percent of single mothers also move in the year following a divorce (see Sara McLanahan, "Family Structure and Stress: A Longitudinal Comparison of Two-Parent and Female-Headed Families," *Journal of Marriage and the Family*, May 1983, pp. 347–357).

10. U.S. Bureau of the Census, *Household and Family Characteristics, March 1987*, Current Population Reports, Series P-20, No. 437, Washington, D.C.: U.S. Government Printing Office, 1988.

11. Garfinkel and McLanahan, *Single Mothers*, p. 1.

12. L. Bumpass, "Children and Marital Disruption: A Replication and Update," *Demography*, Vol. 21 (February 1984), pp. 71–82.

13. Garfinkel and McLanahan reported that average AFDC monthly caseloads for female-headed families declined from about 55 percent in the mid 1970s to about 46 percent in the early 1980s (*Single Mothers*, Table 10, p. 138). In 1990, the last year for which the data are available, the percentage was 47 (U.S. House of Representatives, *1991 Green Book*, Table 19, p. 618, and Table 2, p. 951). For underreporting on the Current Population Survey, see U.S. Bureau of the Census, *Poverty in the United States: 1987*, Current Population Reports, Consumer Income Series P-60, No. 163, 1989, Appendix C.
14. U.S. House of Representatives, *1991 Green Book*, Table 7, p. 598.
15. Lawrence M. Mead, *Beyond Entitlement: The Social Obligations of Citizenship*, New York: Free Press, 1986.
16. Garfinkel and McLanahan, *Single Mothers*, p. 165.
17. Legal scholars distinguish between legal and physical custody. The former refers to decision-making rights of parents; the latter, to the parent with whom the child lives. The parent with physical custody of the child is the resident parent, and the parent without physical custody of the child is the nonresident parent.
18. In some societies, kin networks share responsibility with natural parents for childrearing (see Constantina Safilios-Rothschild, *The Role of the Family: A Neglected Aspect of Poverty*, Washington, D.C.: World Bank Paper #403, 1980; Helen Ware, *Women, Education and Modernization of the Family in West Africa*, Canberra: Australia National University, 1981).
19. Peter Dopffel "Child Support in Europe: A Comparative Overview," in *Child Support: From Debt Collection to Social Policy* (pp. 176–223), edited by Alfred J. Kahn and Sheila B. Kamerman, Newbury Park, Calif.: Sage Publications, 1988, p. 177.
20. For the best single description, see Harry D. Krause, *Child Support in America: The Legal Perspective*, Charlottesville, Va.: Michie Company Law Publishing, 1981). For flavor, see David Chambers, *Making Fathers Pay: The Enforcement of Child Support*, Chicago: University of Chicago Press, 1979. For numbers, see Judith Cassetty, *Child Support and Public Policy: Securing Support from Absent Fathers*, Lexington, Mass.: D.C. Heath and Company, 1978.
21. Cassetty, *Child Support and Public Policy*; Chambers, *Making Fathers Pay*; Irwin Garfinkel and Marygold Melli, editors, "Child Support: Weaknesses of the Old and Features of a Proposed New System," Vol. 1, Institute for Research on Poverty Special Report #32A, Madison, Wis.: University of Wisconsin-Madison, 1982; Isabel V. Sawhill, "Developing Normative Standards for Child Support Payments," in *The Parental Child Support Obligation* (pp. 79–114), edited by Judith Cassetty, Lexington, Mass.: D.C. Heath and Company, 1983.
22. Kenneth R. White and R. Thomas Stone, "A Study of Alimony

and Child Support Rulings with Some Recommendations," *Family Law Quarterly*, Vol. 10, No. 1 (Spring 1976), p. 83; Lucy M. Yee, "What Really Happens in Child Support Cases: An Empirical Study of the Establishment and Enforcement of Child Support Awards in the Denver District Court," *Denver Law Journal*, Vol. 57, No. 1, 1979, p. 21.

23. Chambers, *Making Fathers Pay*.
24. Cassetty, *Child Support and Public Policy*; Garfinkel and Melli, "Child Support."
25. Garfinkel and McLanahan, *Single Mothers*.
26. David Ellwood, "Targeting 'Would Be' Longterm Recipients of AFDC," Mathematica Policy Research Report to U.S. Department of Health and Human Services, Contract #100-84-10059, 1986.
27. Government laws, according to traditional conservatives and many twentieth-century American liberals, are supposed to tell people how to behave. For a discussion of the traditional conservative viewpoint as applied to welfare policy, see Mead, *Beyond Entitlement*. For a different conservative, or more appropriately, nineteenth-century liberal view see Milton Friedman, *Capitalism and Freedom*, Chicago: University of Chicago Press, 1982. American liberals are quite comfortable with laws proscribing racial and gender discrimination, and some are even comfortable with laws encouraging or even requiring affirmative action with respect to minorities and women. At the same time, liberals are uncomfortable with laws telling people how to behave with respect to private family matters such as abortion and birth control.
28. Irwin Garfinkel and Marieka Klawitter, "The Effects of Routine Income Withholding of Child Support on AFDC Participation and Costs," *Journal of Policy Analysis and Management*, Vol. 9, No. 2 (Spring 1990), pp. 155–177; A. Nichols-Casebolt and M. Klawitter, "Child Support Enforcement Reform: Can It Reduce the Welfare Dependency of Never Married Mothers?" Institute for Research on Poverty, Discussion Paper #89-589, University of Wisconsin-Madison, 1989; D. R. Meyer, "Child Support and Welfare Dependency in Wisconsin," unpublished dissertation at the University of Wisconsin-Madison, 1990; D. R. Meyer, I. Garfinkel, P. K. Robins, and D. T. Oellerich, "The Costs and Effects of a National Child Support Assurance System," unpublished paper, 1991.
29. Many scholars place the date much earlier, for example 1535 (see Karl De Schweinitz, *England's Road to Security*, New York: A. S. Barnes and Company, 1975).
30. Adam Smith, *The Wealth of Nations*, New York: Random House, 1965, pp. 135–140.
31. George F. Gilder, *Wealth and Poverty*, New York: Bantam Books, 1981, pp. 140–141.
32. The full picture is even more complicated. The text ignores the

children who have at least one living natural parent but live with neither.

33. J. A. Sweet and L. L. Bumpass, *American Families and Households,* New York: Russell Sage Foundation, 1987.

34. This is because a large proportion of nonresident fathers of children potentially eligible for child support either are not asked or do not inform survey researchers that they have a child living elsewhere. Indeed, Professor Andrew Cherlin of Johns Hopkins University discovered that only about half as many living nonresident fathers were identified in the June 1980 Current Population Survey as resident mothers were identified in the 1979 March–April survey.

35. The tendency of like to mate with like is called *assortative mating.* Over 98 percent of whites mate with whites, and the same is true for blacks (Sweet and Bumpass, *American Families and Households,* chap. 2). The overwhelming majority of men and women mate with partners of similar age. On average, husbands are about three years older than their wives. Marriage within educational class is also pretty strong. It is true that, on occasion, men and women of very different backgrounds mate. It is also true that these couples are more apt to split. But the split is as likely to occur if the man has more or less education than the woman. Thus, even the average backgrounds of fathers and mothers who are unalike as couples tend to be alike.

2 / The Failure of Child Support in the United States

With the Family Support Act of 1988 the United States took meaningful steps toward changing its child support system, moving toward adoption of the Child Support Assurance System. Although the government has been clearly committed to reforming the child support system since the Child Support Enforcement Amendments of 1975, legislative steps have been small ones, significant in their direction toward a long-term objective but insignificant in substantially changing the existing system. The 1988 act shows a strong commitment to overhauling child support in America.

This act focuses on two points: reforming the child support system and expanding work programs and requirements for AFDC recipients. The child support reforms have three specific goals: to increase the number of awards among children who are eligible for child support, to develop guidelines for determining the size of the awards, and to strengthen procedures for collecting the money that is owed—all of which are steps toward adoption of the CSAS.

Although most public attention has focused on the work provisions in the Family Support Act, the child support provisions are far more likely to have an impact on the well-being of the nation's children. As noted in chapter 1, child support reform has implications for at least one of every two children in the United States. The work provisions, on the other hand, are relevant only for families on welfare and affect less than a quarter of all children.[1]

The fact that half of our nation's children will become eligible for child support at some point in the next decade always shocks. When one considers the increased rates of divorce and out-of-wedlock births in America, however, the figure makes sense. There are more single mothers raising children than ever before, and, presumably, most of the children in these homes have fathers who could be contributing to their upbringing. Perhaps the more puzzling point where child support is concerned is how and why our government became so concerned about what happens to children from single-parent homes. To understand how the government's role in child support has grown, it is helpful to look at how the child support system is set up and how it evolved.

THE AMERICAN CHILD SUPPORT SYSTEM

The current American child support system has two components, public and private. The distinction between the two depends on who is paying. Private child support obligations are paid by non-resident parents; public support is paid by the government in the form of AFDC benefits, food stamps, and Medicaid.

Historically, private child support in the United States has been a state responsibility, implemented locally through the courts. A woman who seeks payment of child support from the father of her offspring must go to court to get an award. This is generally done as part of a divorce, a separation, or a paternity proceeding. Because going to court can be an expensive process, few poor or near-poor mothers have awards; most child support awards are held by divorced or separated mothers. Mothers on AFDC must assign their right to a child support award to the state. The welfare department is then responsible for obtaining awards from fathers, and mothers are required to assist in this process. Mothers are allowed to keep the first fifty dollars of payments made by fathers; the rest is used to offset the cost of their AFDC benefits.

HISTORY OF THE FEDERAL GOVERNMENT'S INVOLVEMENT IN PRIVATE CHILD SUPPORT

Single mothers make up the majority of households eligible for child support awards, and most single-mother households are poor or near poor. A brief look at the history of the government's treatment of poor single mothers reveals how America's policies toward this group have affected child support policy and reform. From the time of the first colonists, who brought with them the concept of the British poor law, providing support for the destitute has been considered a public responsibility in America.[2] Originally, local governments took responsibility for their own by taxing residents to aid the indigent. (It was not until the twentieth century that responsibility for aiding the poor shifted from local to state to federal government.)

It was also an early American concern, however, that too much generosity toward the poor would create dependence. As Benjamin Franklin, in a discussion of the British poor law, criticized: "You offered a premium for the encouragement of idleness, and you should not wonder that it has had its effect in the increase of poverty."[3] From the beginning, the United States has struggled to devise systems that will aid the poor without removing the motivation for independent living.

Under the poor law, widows and their children were treated better than other families headed by single women and the rest of the poor. Widows actually were the majority of poor single mothers at the time; divorce, separation, and out-of-wedlock births were discouraged by law and custom and were uncommon. By the time of the American Revolution, pension programs for war widows and their children had been established in most colonies. Expanded pension programs were created for war widows after the Civil War.

Despite the preferential treatment of widows they, as well as other poor single mothers, were expected to earn a living. Many tried to work out of their homes by taking in piecework or boarders, so they could earn income while caring for their children. Those who were unable to combine their work with child care were often forced to place their children in orphanages.

It was not until the early 1900s and the dawning of the Progressive Era that states sought to remedy this situation by enacting mothers' pension programs, so that poor mothers could stay home and raise their children instead of being forced to work. Juvenile court justices, settlement house workers like Jane Addams, public welfare officials, and, ultimately, President Theodore Roosevelt led the reform movement. Between 1910 and 1920, forty states, plus the territories of Alaska and Hawaii, enacted mothers' pension laws.[4] The first such law in Illinois contained a broad definition of dependent children that included deserted families and unwed mothers. This law was so controversial that most of the other early laws restricted aid solely to widows (though aid was extended to all widows, not just war widows, as had previously been the case). Whereas some state laws did include unwed mothers and divorcees, as of 1931, widows constituted 82 percent of those being aided.[5]

In 1935, the federal government followed the states' lead in providing for poor mothers and their children. As part of the landmark Social Security Act, Congress, at the urging of President Franklin Delano Roosevelt, enacted the Aid to Dependent Children program. The federal government's definition of dependent children went further than most state pension programs and explicitly included children of divorced, separated, and never-married mothers, in addition to widows. (In 1951 benefits were added for the custodial parent, as well as the children, and the name of the program was changed to Aid to Families with Dependent Children.)

The new program, like mothers' pensions, was designed to enable poor single mothers to imitate the childrearing practices of the middle class, and, at the turn of the century, few *married* mothers worked for wages. The numbers of women working were still so small, in fact, that the architects who crafted Social Security legislation had no indication that a steady trend toward more women entering the labor force had already begun.

Even though the 1935 Social Security Act created three new federal relief programs (Aid to the Blind, Old Age Assistance, and Aid to Dependent Children), the government's goal remained not only to provide relief to those in need, but also to prevent as many people as possible from needing it. Indeed, President Roosevelt called cash relief a dangerous narcotic.[6] In an attempt to get women off welfare, survivors insurance was created in 1939. This non-income-tested benefit was less stigmatizing than AFDC and provided fewer disincentives to work and remarry. It was eventually successful in getting most widows off welfare.

However, by 1960 it was apparent that, in spite of survivors insurance, AFDC was not withering away. Divorce, separation, and out-of-wedlock births were increasing relative to widowhood. Consequently, survivors' insurance was providing protection to an increasingly smaller proportion of the population of needy children.

The increasing dependence of single mothers on welfare, combined with the increasing number of women in the work force began to spark a policy shift back toward the pre–twentieth century view that poor single mothers should work. This shift began in 1962, when President John F. Kennedy induced Congress to fund social services, such as child care and counseling for welfare mothers, to facilitate welfare recipients' transition to independence. By 1967, however, the still-increasing caseloads made it clear that the social services solution was not working, so Congress turned to the economics profession for a solution and implemented work incentives. These reforms reduced the 100 percent tax rate on earnings of AFDC recipients by allowing them to keep the first thirty dollars of what they made and a third of every dollar after that. In this way, the government hoped to induce welfare recipients to work and become independent. The number of welfare recipients who worked did increase, but total caseloads continued to grow. So in 1972 Congress shifted its reform efforts to an emphasis on work requirements, consisting mainly of mandatory vocational training. Without jobs available, however, such requirements have also proved ineffectual. Nonetheless, Democrats and Republicans continue to seek methods to increase work and to reduce welfare dependence among single mothers.[7] This view is represented most recently in the expanded work requirements of the Family Support Act of 1988.

By the mid-1970s, the expanding caseload of the AFDC program and the shift of that caseload from orphans to children with living, absent parents finally sparked federal interest in child support. Senator Russell B. Long of Louisiana persuaded his colleagues to pass legislation to reduce welfare costs and caseloads by strengthening the collection of private child support due to children on welfare. That legislation was the 1975 Child Support Enforcement Amendments. Collecting child support was a way to get fathers to cover some of the costs of AFDC benefits to single mothers and their children. Furthermore, by increasing the number of child support awards paid, the government hoped it could prevent women from falling into poverty and becoming dependent on AFDC in the first place.

Federal interest in child support enforcement was not entirely new. In 1950 Congress had enacted legislation that required state welfare agencies to notify law enforcement officials when a child receiving AFDC benefits had been deserted or abandoned. In 1962, the Social Security amendments included a provision for federal aid for locating absent parents. And in 1965 and 1967 legislation was enacted that required states to enforce child support and establish paternity.[8]

The 1975 Child Support Enforcement Amendments was the first significant legislation because it provided substantial federal funding for a public bureaucracy to enforce private child support payments. It established the federal Office of Child Support Enforcement, required all states to establish state offices of child support enforcement, and provided federal reimbursement for about three-quarters of each state's enforcement costs. Until that point, all public enforcement of private payments had been a state responsibility. The 1975 amendments provided federal funding to states for nonwelfare recipients only through 1976, but, after a series of temporary extensions, in 1980 Congress permanently extended federal support to all children eligible for private support, irrespective of income and AFDC status. In short, it was the federal government's first step toward paying for and overseeing enforcement of private child support.

Putting this plan into action was a different matter. Because child support had traditionally been a state and local function, the states were, not surprisingly, left with a great deal of latitude in setting up this new enforcement bureaucracy. Unfortunately, no one at the state or federal levels was confident about how to actually strengthen public enforcement of private child support. In fact, most states have proceeded only very gradually to provide child support services to resident parents not receiving welfare.

In 1979, when the U.S. Census Bureau began gathering data on child support to study the effectiveness of the 1975 reforms and determine what remained to be done, they found that many eligible women were still not receiving support. Slightly more than 80 percent of divorced and remarried mothers had awards, about half of separated mothers had awards, and only about 10 percent of never-married mothers had awards. All told, in 1978 (the year the census covered), more than half of the women potentially eligible for child support received nothing.[9]

The U.S. child support system is still failing many of the nation's children. Some of them are living in poverty because child support was never awarded; some are living in poverty because the payments are not collected. Many are living lives of insecurity because of irregular payments; still others, although not in poverty, are living insecurely because of drastic drops in income. The federal government has increasingly required states to adopt more efficient techniques for establishing awards and enforcing payments, but change takes place slowly. Even with reform, weaknesses of the system have lingering effects.

WEAKNESSES OF THE U.S. CHILD SUPPORT SYSTEM AND ATTEMPTED REFORMS

Public Enforcement of Private Awards

Most states have an explicit statement in their divorce statutes of the obligation to pay child support, although in some it is only implied.[10] Child support can also be obtained by going to court for separation agreements or by filing a paternity suit, all family-court procedures. Under the traditional family-court system, three steps are involved in obtaining private child support: (1) identification and location of the nonresident parent, (2) determination of the amount of the award, and (3) payment of child support to the resident parent. The first two steps are done through the courts during divorce, separation, or paternity proceedings. Collection is left largely to the resident parent, who must seek assistance from the courts if the nonresident parent fails to pay the award.

Since 1975, of course, nonresident parents with private awards have also been able to seek assistance through the Office of Child Support Enforcement (OSCE).

There are problems with each step that contribute to the failure of America's child support system to assure that women get the awards they need. The following sections will explain the weaknesses of the child support system and discuss what steps the federal government has taken to try to remedy these problems.

Identification and Location of the Nonresident Parent

In divorce and separation cases, identification of the nonresident parent is seldom difficult. State laws strongly presume that a husband is the father of his wife's children; in some states the law actually prohibits any challenge of this presumption.[11] So, except for the small minority of joint-custody cases in which the child resides part-time with each parent, once physical custody is awarded to one parent, the other is automatically identified as the nonresident parent.

When a mother is unwed, however, a court must establish paternity before a child support obligation can be imposed. Although in the majority of cases the mother knows who the father is, in some there is more than one possibility, and occasionally a mother may falsely name someone as the father. Men who are named as fathers are entitled to contest the allegation. Increasingly, blood tests are used to resolve paternity disputes. A blood test can establish with certainty that a person is not the father of a given child; it can also determine, with relatively high probability, whether a person *is* the father of a given child. Courts used to admit blood test evidence only to exclude paternity, but by 1988 thirty-four states had directed courts to admit blood tests as probabilistic evidence that an alleged father was the actual father.[12] This reform has given unwed mothers a better chance at establishing paternity.

In certain cases, the paternity requirement can be a deterrent to a woman eligible for a child support award. Although most mothers want to identify the father to obtain child support, this is not always the case. Some women, for instance, may not want to have anything to do with the fathers once their children are born. Some fathers, not wanting any legal obligations to a child, may have threatened and warned the mothers not to identify them. Or a woman may not want to jeopardize the relationship by identifying the father. She may feel she can get more out of him informally than by trying to establish a child support award.

Even after an absent parent has been identified, locating him can be a problem. In paternity cases, the alleged father must be informed of his right to contest the allegation. Although it is possible to satisfy these notification requirements by demonstrating good-faith efforts, if the nonresident parent cannot be located, it is obviously impossible to establish and enforce a child support order.

I should note that, because most unwed mothers are poor and on welfare, most questions of paternity are handled by welfare departments, which are responsible for collecting support from the fathers to help offset the costs of AFDC benefits.

Recent reforms. In 1984 Congress passed a law containing two provisions aimed at making paternity establishment easier. The first allows paternity to be established until the child's eighteenth birthday. The second, and more important, provision encourages states to develop administrative or bureaucratic processes to replace judicial processes for establishing paternity. If establishing paternity were a routine procedure that occurred when a mother filled out her child's birth certificate at the hospital, for example, lengthy court procedures to establish paternity could be avoided.

The Family Support Act of 1988 offers three major provisions to strengthen paternity establishment. The first requires states to increase the number of cases in which they establish paternity, by either establishing paternity in at least half of the AFDC out-of-wedlock cases or increasing the proportion of such cases in which they establish paternity by three percentage points each year. Second, states must obtain the social security number of both parents in conjunction with the issuance of birth certificates. This strengthens the 1984 legislation, which merely urged states toward such procedures. Third, all parties in a contested paternity case must take a genetic blood test upon the request of any party, and the federal government will pay 90 percent of the cost of the test.

Determination of the Amount of the Award

The second stage in the child support enforcement process is the establishment of the award. Prior to 1975, judges were given wide latitude in determining the amount of a child support award. In some jurisdictions, judges used numerical standards for determining child support obligations. Nearly every county in Michigan, for example, used a standard in which the child support obligation of the nonresident parent depended only upon his own income and the number of children owed support.[13] Delaware had also developed a numerical standard, though it was far more complicated in that it incorporated many additional factors. Such child support standards were the exception rather than the rule, however.

This does not mean that judges shaped child support agreements completely on a whim. Some states had specific judicial guidelines listed in their divorce laws. For example, Wisconsin's statute as of 1983 instructed courts to apply the following criteria in determining the amount of support: (1) the financial resources of the child; (2) the financial resources of the parents; (3) the standard of living the child would have enjoyed had the marriage not ended in annulment, divorce, or legal separation; (4) the desirability that the custodian remain in the home as a full-time parent; (5) the cost of day care if the custodian works outside the home, or the value of services performed by the custodian if she remains in the home; (6) the physical and emotional health needs of the child; (7) the child's educational needs; (8) the tax consequences to each party; and (9) such other factors as the court may, in each case, determine to be relevant.[14] Generally, child support obligations extended through the child's minority, which by the 1980s had been lowered from age 21 to age 18 in most states. In a few states the nonresident parent was held responsible for a share of the cost of sending his children to college.

In practice, however, judicial discretion usually meant that judges simply rubber-stamped agreements hammered out by the divorcing parents out-of-court.[15] If the parents had sufficient income, they would each hire a lawyer and the lawyers would work out the agreement.

In principle, child support orders could be modified later in response to substantial changes in circumstances, but legislation and judicial practice, not to mention cost, made this extremely difficult. The explicit intention of divorce law was to discourage "unwarranted harassment of the supporting parent by the custodial parent and wasteful use of court facilities."[16]

In analyzing taxes, economists distinguish between horizontal and vertical equity. The former refers to treating equals equally; the latter refers to the relative treatment of the rich and the poor. Numerous studies have documented that the American child support system has failed on both counts, treating equals unequally and engaging in preferential treatment.[17]

Examples of horizontal inequities abound. One study of the Denver court system began with a description of three child support cases, each involving two children. In the first case the nonresident parent's net income was equal to $450 per month, and the child support award was $60 per month. In the second case, the nonresident parent's income was $900 per month, but the child support award was only $50. In the third case, the nonresident parent's income was again equal to $450 per month, but the child support award was $120 a month.[18] Why was the nonresident parent with the highest income ordered to pay the least? Why was the nonresident parent of the third case, with exactly the same income as the first, ordered to pay twice as much? After searching the divorce records, the author concluded that there were no objective factors in the case files that could account for such differences.

Data from divorce cases in Wisconsin in the early 1980s indicate that child support awards ranged from zero to over 100 percent of the nonresident father's income. Awards also varied substantially across counties, with the average award for one child ranging from 12 percent to 24 percent of the nonresident parent's income, depending on the county. For two and three children, the average award ranged from 18 percent to 36 percent, and 13 percent to 37 percent, respectively.[19]

In the early 1980s, I visited a midwestern county that had a reputation for running an effective child support program. One judge heard the bulk of the child support cases. If nonresident parents failed to pay support, he quickly threw them in jail. He was referred to as the "hanging judge." One morning I met with a woman who had been divorced for seven years and had not collected any child support. She complained that she had had the misfortune of scheduling her divorce hearing when the hanging judge was on vacation. The judge she drew had a different philosophy. Although her former husband was making $30,000 to $40,000 per year, he refused to pay child support, telling her she should go on welfare. On several occasions she had brought him to court, and the judge had chastised him. Although he promised the judge he would pay, he never did, and nothing happened. She thought it unfair that, through the luck of the draw, she had not gotten the hanging judge. After lunch I visited two men who were in jail for failure to pay support. They thought it unfair that they had had the ill fortune to have drawn the hanging judge. Both the men and the woman were right: This vast difference in treatment is unfair. This story illustrates the most extreme form of inequality in the old child support enforcement system. Although highly particular, the phenomenon was common.

In addition to treating equals unequally, the old child support system tended to treat nonresidential fathers better than residential mothers and children. The standard of living of nonresident fathers is substantially higher than that of resident mothers and their children. After divorce, the average income of mothers and children is $13,500 for whites and $9,000 for nonwhites, as compared with $25,000 for white nonresident fathers and $13,600 for nonwhite fathers.[20] There is much dispute about the extent to which child support should diminish or eliminate this disparity. However, when one compares the current awards, based on the standards that have been most widely adopted since the Child Support Enforcement Amendments of 1984, child support awards under the old system were only about one-half to two-thirds of what they should be.[21]

Finally, child support obligations within the male population were regressive. That is, they were a greater proportion of the incomes of low-income, nonresident fathers than of those who were well-off. In 1985, nonresident parents with incomes between $5,000 and $10,000 had awards equal to 20 percent of their income. This proportion declined steadily to 9 percent of income for those with incomes in excess of $30,000. This regressivity is offset to some extent by the fact that lower-income, nonresident parents are less likely to be legally required to pay child support than are higher-income parents. (For every $1,000 increase in the income of a nonresident parent, the probability of having a child support obligation increases by 5.4 percent.)[22] But requiring a smaller proportion of low-income parents to pay child support is hardly an equitable way of compensating for the fact that the low-income parents who are required to pay support bear a heavier burden relative to their incomes than do more well-to-do parents.

Recent changes. In an attempt to make the child support system more equitable, the Child Support Enforcement Amendments of 1984 required states to adopt numeric child support guidelines, which courts could use to determine child support obligations. Although the amendments allowed the courts to ignore the guidelines, the Family Support Act of 1988 made the guidelines the presumptive child support award, meaning that departures from the guidelines must be justified in writing and are subject to review by a higher court. Furthermore, the Family Support Act requires that, by 1993, states review child support awards being handled by the Office of Child Support Enforcement (these cases are known as *IV-D cases*) at least every three years and that the Department of Health and Human Services study the impact of requiring periodic review of all child support cases.

Payment of Child Support to the Resident Parent

The third stage of the private child support process is the actual payment of support. Since 1975, all states have required that child support payments due to children on welfare be paid to the state welfare department. In a few states, such as Michigan and Wisconsin, private child support has long been paid through government agencies, which keep track of whether it is paid and then forward payments to resident parents and children.[23] The Michigan Friend of the Court, founded in 1917, is the oldest such agency. Although it had the authority to initiate legal action when obligations were not met, in practice, government agencies that collect private support did not use this authority unless the resident parent specifically requested the office to do so (or unless government subsidies to the resident family were involved). In most states, people with private awards had to seek their own remedy for nonpayment of child support.

Thus, in the vast majority of nonwelfare cases, the burden of collecting overdue support falls on the resident parent alone. The standard procedure is for the court to order the nonresident parent to pay, leaving the beneficiary of the order, the resident parent, responsible for collection. This means that, if the nonresident parent fails to pay, the resident parent has to initiate a legal action, usually by citing the nonresident parent for contempt. This proceeding is fraught with difficulties. It usually requires legal counsel, which is a substantial financial burden for a parent not receiving support. And providing adequate records to prove that no payment is being made can be difficult when private payments are made directly to the resident parent. Although the enforcement services of the Office of Child Support Enforcement have been extended to nonwelfare cases since 1975, only a small proportion of nonwelfare resident parents have taken advantage of them.

When a resident parent did bring a nonresident parent to court for not meeting his obligation, a variety of options were available to the judge, such as imposing liens or sentencing the nonpayor to jail. The most effective tool for collecting child support was a wage assignment.[24] A wage assignment, also known as a garnishment, is a legal order to the employer of the nonresident parent to withhold the child support from the employee's wages. Until the early 1980s, however, wage assignments were used only infrequently as a response to late payment.

Jail was the ultimate sanction for those who didn't pay. But because the decision of what to do with a nonresident parent who failed to pay was also left to judges, this too was inequitably imposed. Thousands of nonresident parents have been jailed each year in Michigan alone for failure to comply with child support orders.[25] But, on a national level, only a tiny minority of nonresident parents who fail to pay child support are jailed.

When the parents of a child live in different states, enforcement of child support obligations was, and still is, particularly difficult for many legal and bureaucratic reasons, not the least of which is that different jurisdictions often have different laws. The weakness of interstate child support enforcement is important because approximately one-third of cases are interstate.[26]

Recent reforms. The Child Support Enforcement Amendments of 1984 required states to withhold child support obligations from wages and other income sources of nonresident parents who became one-month delinquent in their payments of child support. The 1988 Family Support Act immensely strengthened the 1984 withholding provisions. It requires withholding of the child support obligation from the outset for all cases served by state child support offices as of 1990 and for all child support cases as of 1994, not just cases of delinquency.

Further, whereas the 1984 amendments urged states to develop more efficient techniques to enforce child support when the father is in a different state, the 1988 act offers financial incentive to states to undertake such demonstrations and also establishes a federal advisory council to make recommendations for future legislation on interstate enforcement of child support.

AFDC BENEFITS AS PUBLIC CHILD SUPPORT

Public transfers to poor families with children eligible for child support substantially exceed private child support transfers to all U.S. children. Whereas slightly over $7 billion in private child support was paid in 1985, expenditures for single-mother families in the AFDC, Medicaid, food stamps, and housing assistance programs equaled $24 billion, or more than three times private child support.[27] AFDC is the largest of the public programs that provides benefits to children potentially eligible for child support. In 1988, the average monthly caseload in the AFDC program consisted of 3.7 million families with 7.3 million children.[28] Although the program aids children of widows and children in two-parent families when the father is unemployed or disabled, these two groups represent only 13 percent of the families aided.[29] The overwhelming majority of families receiving AFDC consist of mothers living with children who have nonresident fathers.

HOW PUBLIC SUPPORT WORKS

The system for obtaining public child support awards differs from the private system in that mothers who receive AFDC benefits must assign their rights to child support to the state. In addition, they must cooperate with state officials to identify and locate the fathers of their children. As noted earlier, the family is entitled to receive up to $50 per month of the child support paid by the nonresident parent, and all additional child support paid by the nonresident parent is kept by the state to offset the AFDC benefit.

In fiscal year 1988, the cost of the AFDC program was $17 billion. Of this amount, $9.3 billion, or a bit more than half, was paid for by the federal government. The states and, in a few cases, the counties, paid for the rest. So, although states determine benefit levels and administer the programs, the federal government is still covering most of the welfare bill. It makes sense, therefore, for the government to be interested in enforcing child support, for it could be a revenue source for reducing the AFDC bill.

WEAKNESSES OF PUBLIC CHILD SUPPORT IN REGARD TO CHILD SECURITY

When the AFDC program was enacted in 1935 as part of the Social Security Act, the overwhelming majority of single mothers still were widows, and, as noted, mothers of young children were not expected to work outside the home. Today, the overwhelming majority of families aided by AFDC have a living nonresident parent, and the resident parent is increasingly expected to work. Partly because of this disjuncture between original and current objectives and partly because welfare programs always spark controversy, AFDC and the other welfare programs that accompany it are now subject to intense criticism.[30]

Nearly everyone is critical of welfare. It is criticized from the Left for being inadequate and stigmatizing its beneficiaries. It is criticized from the Right for undermining the family and the work ethic and promoting long-term welfare dependence. Each of these criticisms has some merit.

Why Welfare is Inadequate and Discourages Work

Current welfare benefits *are* inadequate. From about 1955–1975 U.S. policymakers turned their attention to preventing poverty and reducing insecurity. In the half decade following President Johnson's declaration of a War on Poverty, the generosity of the welfare package was increased dramatically. Benefits went up, Medicaid and food stamps were added, and, for the first time since AFDC was enacted, the benefits actually approached a level at which women with children could survive on AFDC payments, even in places like New York City. In short, America achieved a substantial reduction in poverty. At the same time, the proportion of all single mothers receiving welfare also increased from about 45 percent to 65 percent.

The real value of the welfare benefit package, however, has been falling steadily since 1975, due to inflation and the decision, resulting from alarm over growing dependence, not to raise benefit levels. Benefits in 1988 were 25 percent lower than they had been in 1975.[31] The current average benefit from AFDC and food stamps combined is equal to less than three-fourths of the poverty line.[32] With the cut in benefits, the proportion of single-mother families on welfare did drop to 45 percent, but child poverty also increased by about a third.

A comparison with the treatment of the aged provides an indicator of the inadequacy of welfare benefits for female-headed families with children. The federal benefits received by an aged couple are equal to at least 100 percent of the poverty line, and twenty-one states pay even higher benefits.[33]

The stigma associated with welfare stems from the sharp cleavage AFDC creates between taxpayers and mothers aided by welfare. Those who receive the aid are often looked down upon as lazy and dependent, a view of themselves that some welfare mothers come to accept. In the United States, where so much stress is put on economic success and where the dominant ideology is that "with hard work, anyone can make it," to declare oneself poor is tantamount to declaring oneself a failure.[34]

Why Welfare Discourages Regular Work and Encourages Dependency

The public transfer programs available to poor single mothers have one thing in common: They provide benefits to only families with low incomes. Income eligibility levels are, for the most part, below the poverty line. In a few states, because of deductions for work-related expenses, it is possible to remain on AFDC with incomes slightly above the poverty level. Despite all the attention such cases have received, however, they are rare. Families eligible for AFDC are also automatically eligible for medical assistance through the Medicaid program. In addition, nearly all AFDC families are eligible for food stamps, which may be used in lieu of money to purchase food. Finally, about 20 percent of AFDC families also live in public housing or receive public rent subsidies.[35] Taken together, AFDC, food stamps, and Medicaid put a floor under the income of most families with children who are eligible for child support. As of January 1989, the AFDC and food stamp benefits for a mother and two children ranged from a low of $346 per month in Mississippi to a high of $782 per month in California, or from 45 percent to 100 percent of the poverty level for a family of three.[36]

AFDC benefits eliminate 12 percent of the poverty gap (the difference between a family's income and the poverty line for that family) of female-headed families.[37] If in-kind benefits including Medicaid, food stamps, and public housing are counted, the percentage reduction in the poverty rate is nearly 44 percent for white female heads and 33 percent for nonwhite female heads.[38]

But, to confine eligibility for these programs to low-income families, benefits are reduced as other income increases. Benefits in the AFDC program are reduced by $1 for each dollar of unearned income. The first $50 per month of child support does not result in a reduction in AFDC benefits. Earned income is treated somewhat more generously. Work-related expenses of up to $70 per month, plus up to $160 per month for child-care expenses, plus an additional $30 per month are first subtracted from earnings. Benefits are then reduced by one dollar for each dollar of earnings in excess of these deductions. In addition, for the first four months of work, one-third of all earnings are ignored in calculating benefits. Benefits in the food stamp program are reduced by about thirty cents for each dollar of other income. Taken together, the benefit reduction rates in the AFDC and food stamp programs average about 75 percent: Mothers who go to work lose about three-quarters of their welfare and food stamp benefits. Moreover, if a mother on AFDC can earn enough to leave welfare, she will lose not only her AFDC benefits but also her Medicaid benefits.

By reducing benefits as earnings increase, welfare discourages work. And because they lose their Medicaid and food stamp benefits and their AFDC benefits when they go to work, welfare mothers with limited education and little prospect of earning much more than the minimum wage find it unprofitable to work. For those at the bottom of the income distribution—women who can't earn very much money—welfare does become a long-term dependency. That would not be the case if supporting institutions outside of welfare were better and provided adequate services such as child support and medical care. When such families can't get decent medical care or child support, it doesn't pay for them to work. Too many remain on welfare.

Disadvantages of Dependency

About 30 percent of the single mothers who ever receive benefits spend no more than two years on welfare. But another 40 percent receive benefits for three to seven years, and another 30 percent receive benefits for eight or more years.[39] Because long-term recipients (in the third category) are more likely to be receiving benefits at any particular time, they represent a large share of the caseload, about 65 percent of the total in any given month. At this point we have no knowledge about the extent to which those dependent on welfare for eight or more years are healthy or disabled or mix earnings with welfare.

What effects will this long-run dependence have on single mothers and their children? Many people believe that welfare harms beneficiaries by undermining their motivation to escape poverty and make a better life for themselves. Some even argue that it creates a "culture" of poverty and dependence that is passed on from one generation to the next.

There is some evidence of intergenerational dependence, but

the interpretation of its cause is ambiguous. No one doubts that poverty breeds poverty, and some intergenerational welfare dependence is a natural consequence of this process. The question is, Does the provision of welfare increase or reduce the extent to which subsequent generations will be poor and dependent? The answer is, We do not know.[40]

At this point social science knowledge is too scanty to warrant either the extreme judgment that welfare does more harm than good or that society does not need to be concerned about the possible ill effects of welfare. Nonetheless, in view of the ambiguity of the evidence and the high value that society places on independence, it is prudent to seek alternative methods of aiding single women with children, methods that will stigmatize them less and reinforce their independence more. The Child Support Assurance System is such a program.

Shortcomings of Welfare Alone

Despite its weaknesses, we will retain some form of welfare for single mothers and their children.[41] Public responsibility for the poor makes capitalism more dynamic. The safety net of welfare programs facilitates the free play of the labor market by protecting people rather than jobs or businesses.

Ironically, the goals of the Left—eliminating the stigma and increasing adequacy—would be easier to achieve if an objective of the Right—reducing welfare dependence—were achieved. First, if fewer people were dependent on welfare, and they used it for a shorter period of time, there would be more political support for increasing the benefits. In other words, if welfare were used only for what it is supposed to be used for—a short-term safety net—society would be more receptive to strengthening the net. As for the stigma, a certain negative connotation inevitably accompanys the receipt of welfare.[42] The contempt is likely to be less strong, however, if the receipt of welfare is temporary. Again, if we want to reduce the negativity of AFDC, we must reduce long-term dependence on it.

AFDC falls short of being a reliable system for assuring that children living without one parent are financially secure. Its most basic failing is that it is not a preventive program. AFDC is of help only after a family falls into poverty. This is not a criticism of AFDC for what it is; it is a criticism of use of it for what it is not. We have come to rely on the welfare safety net to support too many single mothers and their children. As a result, the system is overburdened. The problem is not that welfare programs do not prevent poverty, but rather that our menu of social programs to deal with economic insecurity arising from divorce and nonmarriage is limited. The new child support assurance system is a critical addition to our social security program menu.

SUMMARY

When the public enforcement of private child support was a state responsibility, the system indirectly condoned, and therefore fostered, parental irresponsibility. This, in turn, contributed to poverty and welfare dependence among single-mother families. Furthermore, with states, localities, and, ultimately, judges all determining awards, the system was also highly inequitable.

As for America's public system of child support, welfare is fine if the only aim is to relieve poverty. To prevent poverty and promote independence by having mothers work, however, calls for a different program. Assuring that mothers have child support offers a logical alternative.

In the latest attempt to reduce the growing AFDC caseload and reduce poverty among poor single mothers, the U.S. government has finally begun looking outside of welfare toward a universal system of child support. Recognizing the weaknesses of both public and private child support systems, the government is taking steps to simplify and strengthen both parts by moving toward adoption of the Child Support Assurance System. In the private arena, the CSAS replaces a system characterized by judicial discretion with one of bureaucratic regularity, in the form of universal standards and procedures. As for remedying the weaknesses of the public system, the CSAS was designed with the dual goal of preventing poverty and promoting independence from welfare. So how would this plan deliver on its promises? The next chapter will explain.

NOTES

1. In 1987, 11.4 percent of children below age eighteen received welfare, whereas close to a quarter were eligible for child support. Assuming that the rate of welfare receipt among mothers eligible for child support remains constant, the work provisions of the Family Support Act should affect less than half as many children as do the child support provisions. For information on welfare receipt, see U.S. House of Representatives, Committee on Ways and Means, *Background Material and Data on Programs within the Jurisdiction of the Committee on Ways and Means: 1989 Edition,* Washington, D.C.: U.S. Government Printing Office, 1989, Table 21, p. 560.
2. The material in this section is drawn from Garfinkel and McLanahan, *Single Mothers,* chap. 4.
3. Quoted in Samuel Mencher, *Poor Law to Poverty Programs,* Pittsburgh: University of Pittsburgh Press, 1967, p. 96.
4. For a description of the development of mothers' pension and other aid-to-mother-only families with children, see Emma Octavina Lundberg, *Unto the Least of These,* New York: Appleton-Century Company, 1974. See also W. Bell, *Aid to Dependent Children,* New York: Columbia University Press, 1965; Mark Leff, "Consensus for Reform: The Mothers' Pension Movement in the Progressive Era," *Social Service Review,* Vol. 47, No. 3 (September 1973), pp. 391–417; Helen Slessarev, "From Mothers' Pensions to Aid to Dependent Children: The Legalization of Women's Traditional Role as Childbearer," unpublished document, University of Chicago, Winter 1983.
5. Helen Slessarev, "Women's Traditional Role as Childbearer."
6. President Franklin D. Roosevelt, quoted in Josephine C. Brown, *Public Relief 1929–1939,* New York: Henry Holt and Company, 1940, p. 165.
7. See "Up from Dependency: A New National Public Assistance Strategy," Report to the president by the Domestic Policy Council Low Income Opportunity Working Group, December 1986; "A New Social Contract: Rethinking the Nature and Purpose of Public Assistance," Report of the Task Force on Poverty and Welfare, Submitted to Governor Mario Cuomo, State of New York, December 1986; "Ladders out of Poverty," Report of the Project on the Welfare of Families, edited by J. A. Meyer, 1986.
8. U.S. Department of Health and Human Services, Office of Child Support Enforcement, *Child Support Enforcement,* 5th Annual Report to Congress for the Period Ending September 30, 1980, December 1980.
9. U.S. Bureau of the Census, *Child Support and Alimony: 1978,* Current Population Reports, Special Studies Series P-23, No. 112,

1981. Only 3.2 percent of those without child support awards received property settlements instead (U.S. Bureau of the Census, *Child Support and Alimony: 1983* (Supplemental Report), Current Population Reports, Special Studies Series P-23, No. 148, 1986, Table B). For an analysis of the relative importance of child support and property settlements for the economic well-being of children, see J. A. Seltzer and I. Garfinkel, "Inequality in Divorce Settlements: An Investigation of Property Settlements and Child Support," *Social Science Research*, December, 1989, pp. 82–111. The data reported in the Current Population Survey-Child Support Supplement are from reports by mothers. To the extent that fathers' and mothers' reports diverge, the evidence indicates that the mothers report more accurately (see N. C. Schaeffer, J. A. Seltzer, and M. Klawitter, "Nonresponse and Response Bias: Estimating Resident and Nonresident Parents' Reports about Child Support," *Sociological Methods and Research*, Vol. 20, No. 1 (August 1991), pp. 30–59.

10. D. Krause, *Child Support in America*, p. 3.
11. Ibid., p. 106.
12. D. H. Kaye and R. Kanwischer, "Admissibility of Genetic Testing in Paternity Litigation: A Survey of State Statutes," *Family Law Quarterly*, Vol. 12, No. 2 (Summer 1988), Table 1, pp. 109–116.
13. D. Chambers, *Making Fathers Pay*, p. 39.
14. Wisconsin Statutes: 1983–1984, Vol. 3, chap. 767.25. See also Krause, *Child Support in America*, p. 11.
15. Erlanger and colleagues found that over 90 percent of child support agreements were arrived at by the parties outside of court and rubber-stamped by the judiciary (Howard S. Erlanger, Elizabeth Chambliss, and Marygold S. Melli, "Participation and Flexibility in Informal Process: Cautions from the Divorce Context," *Law and Society Review*, Vol. 21, No. 4, 1987, pp. 585–604). Mnookin and Kornhauser talk about bargaining between former spouses (Robert H. Mnookin and Lewis Kornhauser, "Bargaining in the Shadow of the Law: The Case of Divorce," *Yale Law Journal*, Vol. 88, No. 5 (April 1979), pp. 950–997).
16. Krause, *Child Support in America*, p. 19. As of 1980, the Uniform Marriage and Divorce Act required "a showing of changed circumstances so substantial and continuing as to make the terms (previously set) unconscionable."
17. The two most frequently cited empirical studies on this point are White and Stone, "Study of Alimony and Child Support Rulings," pp. 75–91; L. M. Yee, "What Really Happens in Child Support Cases," pp. 21–70.
18. Yee, "What Really Happens in Child Support Cases," p. 21.
19. Ann Nichols-Casebolt, Irwin Garfinkel, and Patrick Wong, "Reforming Wisconsin's Child Support System," in *State Policy*

Choices: The Wisconsin Experience, edited by Sheldon Danzinger and John F. Witte, Madison, Wis.: University of Wisconsin Press, 1988, pp. 17–64.

20. Ann Nichols-Casebolt, "The Economic Impact of Child Support Reform on the Poverty Status of Custodial and Noncustodial Families," *Journal of Marriage and the Family,* Vol. 48 (November 1986), pp. 875–880.

21. The standards or guidelines are the Wisconsin percentage-of-income standard and the income-shares standard (see Donald T. Oellerich, Irwin Garfinkel, and Philip K. Robins, "Private Child Support: Current and Potential Impacts," *Journal of Sociology and Social Welfare,* Vol. 18, No. 1 (March 1991), p. 20).

22. Patrick Wong, *The Economic Effects of the Wisconsin Child Support Assurance System: A Simulation Study with a Labor Supply Model,* unpublished dissertation at University of Wisconsin-Madison, 1988, Table 5.4, p. 166.

23. By 1984 six other states had also done this: Arizona, Iowa, Nebraska, North Dakota, Oregon, and Pennsylvania (M. Melli, "Child Support: A Survey of the Statutes," Institute for Research on Poverty Special Report Series #33, Madison, Wis.: University of Wisconsin, 1984).

24. Krause, *Child Support in America;* Chambers, *Making Fathers Pay.*

25. Chambers, *Making Fathers Pay,* p. 165.

26. U.S. House of Representatives, *Background Material and Data on Programs,* p. 686.

27. Garfinkel and McLanahan, *Single Mothers,* p. 140.

28. U.S. House of Representatives, *Background Material and Data on Programs,* Table 20, p. 559.

29. About 10 percent of the families have no adult, and a very small percentage have resident fathers and nonresident mothers (see tables 22 and 26 of House of Representatives, *Background Material and Data on Programs*). The 1985 Current Population Survey-Child Support Supplement indicates that there are about 15.2 million children who live with their mothers who are potentially eligible for child support. (The four-or-more-children category was treated as if there were an average of five children in the category.)

30. For a description of the historical controversies surrounding welfare programs see Garfinkel and McLanahan, *Single Mothers,* chap. 4; F. F. Piven and R. A. Cloward, *Regulating the Poor: The Functions of Public Welfare,* New York: Vintage Books, 1971; M. B. Katz, *In the Shadow of the Poorhouse: A Social History of Welfare in America,* New York: Basic Books, 1986.

31. U.S. House of Representatives, *Background Material and Data on Programs,* Table 13, pp. 547–548.

32. Ibid., Table 9, pp. 539–540.

33. Ibid., Tables 5 and 7, pp. 683–684, and 689.

34. For a detailed discussion of the role of stigma in income-tested transfer programs, see Lee Rainwater, "Stigma in Income-Tested Programs," in *Income-Tested Transfer Programs: The Case for and Against,* edited by I. Garfinkel, New York: Academic Press, 1982.

35. U.S. House of Representatives, *Background Material and Data on Programs,* p. 580.

36. Ibid., Table 9, pp. 539–540. Benefits in Alaska, where living costs are extraordinarily high, were even higher at $1,009 per month, or 103 percent of the poverty level.

37. Sheldon Danziger and Peter Gottschalk, "How Have Families with Children Been Faring?" Institute for Research on Poverty Discussion Paper #801-86, Madison, Wis.: University of Wisconsin-Madison, 1986, Table 14.

38. Timothy M. Smeeding, "The Antipoverty Effectiveness of In-kind Transfers," *Journal of Human Resources,* Vol. 12, No. 3, 1977, Table 5, pp. 360–378.

39. Ellwood, "Long-Term Recipients of AFDC," Table II-3, p. 16.

40. Other things being equal, families who receive welfare are poorer than those who do not. This is true even in studies that control for income. It is impossible to control for unmeasured differences between poor families who are and are not on welfare. For a more detailed account, see Garfinkel and McLanahan, *Single Mothers,* pp. 26–43. For a more recent attempt to estimate the intergenerational transmission of welfare, see Peter Gottschalk, "The Intergenerational Transmission of Welfare Participation: Facts and Possible Causes," Institute for Research on Poverty Discussion Paper #925-90, Madison, Wis.: University of Wisconsin-Madison, 1990.

41. For a discussion of reforms of the welfare system, see Garfinkel and McLanahan, *Single Mothers,* pp. 185–187.

42. See the *New York Times* (March 11, 1991, p. 12) for a story by Steven A. Holmes entitled "Once welfare meant someone else, but recession brings home its sting." It describes the shame and stigma felt by men and women from Framingham, Massachusetts, who finally applied for welfare assistance but hid it from their friends, relatives, and neighbors.

3 / A New Child Support Assurance System

HOW THE CHILD SUPPORT ASSURANCE SYSTEM EVOLVED

In 1974, when it became clear that Congress would pass the Child Support Enforcement Amendments, the then Department of Health, Education and Welfare asked the Institute for Research on Poverty (IRP) at the University of Wisconsin to conduct a study of the nation's child support system.[1] At the time, I was director designate of the IRP and persuaded Judith Cassetty, a Ph.D. student in social work, to write a dissertation on the topic. As noted in the Preface, her dissertation, completed in 1977 and published the next year as a book, *Child Support and Public Policy,* was the first piece of child support research conducted at the IRP.

In addition to recounting the historical origins of the Child Support Enforcement Amendments, Cassetty developed estimates of the relative incomes of divorced nonresident and resident parents and of the potential effects on their incomes of different formulas for child support awards. She also examined some of the benefits and costs of the enforcement system that was established by the 1975 Child Support Enforcement Amendments.

One of Cassetty's main recommendations was that the amount of child support awarded should be determined by a legislated, numerical formula, instead of being left to the discretion of each court. Legislated formulas would provide a fairer system overall. The formula she favored was one that equalized the incomes of the two parents. In other words, money should be taken from the father's income until it was equal to the income of the wife and children, Isabel Sawhill, at the Urban Institute had made similar recommendations.[2]

Meanwhile Professor Harold Watts, the first director of IRP, was serving on a Carnegie Foundation panel of national experts that was looking at the economic and social well-being of children. His discussions with Cassetty and his own familiarity with the income tax led him to propose that the income tax be used to help enforce child support. He suggested that, when taxes were filed at the end of the year, nonresident parents who owed child support be required to declare how much they owed and whether or not they had paid that amount.

Building on the ideas of Cassetty, Sawhill, and Watts and on my own research on welfare, in 1977 I proposed the creation of a new child support assurance system (CSAS). In 1980, the state of Wisconsin requested a detailed design for the CSAS, along with an estimate of the costs and benefits of such a plan.

For the next few years I worked with researchers at IRP, in conjunction with civil servants in the Wisconsin Office of Child Support Enforcement, studying weaknesses of the child support system and developing and designing this proposed new child support system. Among others, the group included Judith Cassetty, Tom Corbett, Marygold Melli, Bernard Stumbras, and Sherwood Zink. Corbett was completing a doctoral program in social work at the University of Wisconsin. He had worked for the Department of Health and Social Services, under Stumbras and alongside Zink. So, he became a key liaison between the state and our group. Zink was the legal counsel for the State Office of Child Support. He drafted all of the legislation and was instrumental in garnering local political support. Stumbras, the head of the division of income maintenance, was a career civil servant with the highest executive rating, who was given much of the credit for making Wisconsin the first state in the nation to computerize its welfare record keeping. His involvement assured us, and others within the department and legislature, that we were serious. Marygold Melli, a law professor at the University of Wisconsin, had drafted Wisconsin's juvenile code. She drafted the model law for the Child Support Assurance System we proposed in our 1982 report to the state, *Child Support: Weaknesses of the Old and Features of a Proposed New System.*

Although we used Cassetty's recommendation for a legislated standard to determine the amount of child support that should be paid, rather than equalizing the incomes of both parents, we based the standard on the notion that a nonresident parent should share the same proportion of his income with his child as he would have if he were living with the child. And although Watts's proposal to use the income tax got us thinking about using tax filing to track payments, it did not seem practical as the sole means of enforcement. We believed that withholding the income from nonresident fathers would be more effective.

The other issue we researched in developing a new child support plan was work incentives for single mothers. This was currently the largest group of poor people, certainly a group who could benefit from child support. The desire to encourage these mothers to work was clearly important in any plan that was going to give more money to this group.

Though there have been many proposals to reform our child support system, the CSAS has become the model for national reform. Wisconsin was the first state to start testing it. During the 1980s, Wisconsin adopted a series of laws that took the state gradually toward a new child support assurance system. Concerned about costs, Wisconsin has implemented the system slowly, testing the percentage-of-income standard and routine income withholding before implementing an assured benefit. Thus, the state now has two of the three key elements of the CSAS in place. Unfortunately, due to changes in the political climate, it seems unlikely that it will test an assured benefit. New York, however, is currently piloting a variant of an assured benefit. I will explain the Wisconsin and New York systems in detail at the end of the chapter and discuss what we have learned from these experiments. But first, here is a description of the CSAS.

THE CSAS: ITS STRUCTURE AND RATIONALE

The philosophical premise underlying the CSAS is that parents are responsible for sharing income with their children and government is responsible for assuring that children who live apart from their parents receive the share to which they are entitled. What exactly is the share to which they are entitled? How can it be assured that children receive that share? These are the issues that the CSAS attempts to resolve. The three major components of the system are (1) a child support standard, (2) routine income withholding, and (3) an assured child support benefit.

The Child Support Standard

A child support standard or guideline, that is, a simple numerical formula for establishing the amount of child support obligations, is an essential component of the proposed new child support assurance system. The Child Support Enforcement Amendments of 1984 required the states to develop guidelines in the form of mathematical formulas for use by the courts in setting child support. The Family Support Act of 1988 made those formulas presumptive, that is, it required that courts use them unless a court gives reasons on the record for not doing so.[3] Thus, every state in the country is well on its way to adopting this critical component of the CSAS.

What differs from state to state is the standard that is used. This will become an increasingly debated issue in child support policy in the next few years. The child support standard I recommend is a percentage-of-income standard that depends only on the gross income of the nonresident parent and the number of children to be supported. The formula for the standard is a set percentage rate for one child (17 percent), which is increased if there are more children: 25, 29, 31, and 34 percent, respectively, for two, three, four, and five or more children.

Any legislated standard reduces inequities caused by judicial discretion in awards decisions. The benefit of using the percentage-of-income standard is twofold. First, this formula makes child support awards easy to calculate, understand, and implement. Second, the standard provides automatic indexing of awards, so that, as the income of the nonresident parent increases or decreases, the amount owed automatically increases or decreases, respectively. And because the incomes of most nonresident parents increase over time, a percentage-of-income standard will lead to increased payments to most children. At the same time, it provides greater fairness to the nonresident parent who becomes unemployed or ill: If the earnings of a nonresident parent decrease owing to unemployment or illness, his child support obligation automatically drops.

Routine Income Withholding

The second component of the CSAS is also ideal in its simplicity. Once an award has been determined, the nonresident parent who owes the child support has the award payment withheld from his paycheck. This money goes to the local Office of Child Support and is, in turn, sent to the resident parent each month. This method increases both the size and the timeliness of child support payments. The 1988 Family Support Act requires that all states adopt income withholding laws.

Currently, the average nonresident father pays only 59 percent of the dollars he owes in child support. (Because nonresident parents who owe more pay a higher percentage of what they owe, the amount of total dollars paid out of total dollars owed is 71 percent.) About half of the fathers pay the full amount they owe, another quarter pay part of what they owe, and the last quarter pay nothing.

Nonresident parents who have defaulted for a few months may have spent the money for other purposes and often cannot afford to pay the arrearage. Most important, Wisconsin's experience in the early 1980s with withholding in response to delinquency shows that 70 percent of nonresident parents became delinquent within three years. No society profits by making so many into lawbreakers.

Wisconsin began a trial of routine income withholding in 1984 in ten counties. An evaluation of the experience in these pilot counties and in ten matched comparison counties suggested that routine withholding increased child support payments by between 11 percent and 30 percent.[4] An increase of 11 percent would increase the national amount of child support collections, out of total child support obligations, from 59 percent to 65 percent, whereas an increase of 30 percent would increase the proportion to 77 percent. As the numbers indicate, routine withholding could have a substantial impact on the effectiveness of child support collection. Moreover, routine income witholding of child support obligations is a nonstigmatizing, preventive measure. Because nearly everyone who owes child support is subject to withholding, it not being a punishment for delinquency removes stigma and punishment from the collection process while enhancing children's economic security.

The Assured Child Support Benefit

The third, and currently the most controversial, component of the CSAS is the assured benefit. This part of the plan calls for the caretaker of a child legally entitled to receive private child support to receive either the award money that the nonresident parent pays or an assured child support benefit, whichever is higher. When nonresident parents pay less than the assured child support benefit level, the difference is made up by the government. This benefit would be universal, not income tested. The public-subsidy portion of the assured benefit would count as taxable income for the resident parent. The benefit would last until the child turned nineteen.

I propose that, initially, the benefit for one child be $2,000 to $2,500 per year. This figure represents less than the cost of raising a child, so it still leaves an incentive for the recipient parent to work, but, when combined with earnings and other benefits, it could substantially reduce poverty and insecurity at practically no cost to the public. I also recommend that assured benefits for the second, third, fourth, fifth, and sixth child be equal to $1,000, $1,000, $500, $500, and $500, respectively. These figures take account of economies of scale. Studies indicate that expenditures on a second and third child are about half of the amount devoted to the first.[5]

To maximize the incentive to leave AFDC, the benefits paid out under it would be reduced by one dollar for each dollar of the assured benefit. But the assured child support would not be reduced by any income earned by the resident parent. As a consequence, the assured benefit begins to benefit a family only if the resident parent leaves AFDC and goes to work.

The assured benefit insures all children legally entitled to private child support against the risk that the nonresident parent will fail to pay. This public-insurance feature of the assured benefit nicely complements a child support standard that expresses child support awards as a percentage of income. Because incomes of nonresident parents generally increase over time, the percentage-of-income orders generally benefit resident parents and their children. In some cases, however, the nonresident parent becomes unemployed or ill and his income drops. The percentage-of-income standard automatically protects these nonresident parents by reducing the child support obligation. At the same time, the assured benefit protects the resident parent and children by guaranteeing that child support does not fall to zero.

For the very poorest families, an assured child support benefit is more likely to be a long-term supplement to the private child support paid by the nonresident parent. In such cases, the assured benefit reduces economic insecurity, not only by providing insurance, but also by increasing income.

Reduction of welfare dependence.   An assured child support benefit also reduces welfare dependence. One of the attractions of welfare is that, although benefits are low, they are certain. By reducing economic insecurity, an assured child support benefit makes life outside of welfare more secure and, therefore, more attractive. In addition, because the assured benefit is not reduced dollar for dollar as earnings increase, it provides a greater incentive to work than does welfare. One-half to three-quarters of all welfare recipients cannot command high enough wages to lift their families out of poverty, even if they work full-time year-round.[6] Even with support from their children's fathers, they still would not have enough.[7] Even if child support awards were better enforced, most fathers of AFDC children earn little and, therefore, have little to share with their children. If they are to escape both poverty and welfare dependence, their earnings must be supplemented. An assured child support benefit is an ideal mechanism for supplementing the earnings of single mothers not on welfare, because the benefit is not eliminated as earnings increase.

Incentive to establish paternity.　The widespread failure to establish paternity remains one of the weakest links in the enforcement of private child support. An assured child support benefit creates incentives for unwed mothers, community leaders, and welfare and child support officials to cooperate in the establishment of paternity.[8] Entitlement to an assured child support benefit is dependent upon legal entitlement to private child support, which, in turn, is dependent upon the identification of a liable nonresident parent. In nonmarital cases, that means paternity must be established. Thus, in order to qualify for an assured child support benefit, mothers of children born out of wedlock have to identify the fathers of their children.

An assured child support benefit is also likely to induce community leaders of poor groups to urge their constituents to be more cooperative with respect to paternity establishment. Historically, advocates for the poor have not looked upon child support enforcement with a great deal of enthusiasm. This is understandable, for, in the presence of AFDC and the absence of an assured benefit, child support enforcement amounts to Robin Hood's economics in reverse: Taking from poor fathers to reduce AFDC costs reduces the tax burden of middle and upper-middle-income families. Of course, if one believes, as I do, that poor fathers should be paying child support, enforcement of this obligation is hardly analogous to stealing. Nevertheless, strengthening enforcement in the absence of an assured benefit does redistribute from poor to rich. The assured benefit mitigates this effect. It is an effective means of reinvesting the savings of increased child support collections. Sharing the gains of increased collections with poor resident-parent families who have child support awards not only bolsters their incomes in times of hardship, but also gives resident parents an incentive to cooperate in establishing paternity and locating the nonresident parents of their children.

A potential positive side effect of the assured benefit, as Professor David Ellwood argues, is that it would strengthen public resolve to hold fathers accountable for supporting their children.

When the public complains about money being spent on the assured benefit, attention will turn to "those damn fathers." Debate will turn on whether they should be required to work or be provided with job training. It is quite possible that the outcome will involve both greater demands of and greater services for poor fathers.

Strengthening child support enforcement has already begun to reduce AFDC costs and will do so even more in the future. The AFDC savings can be used to reduce taxes, but, in view of the fact that children potentially eligible for child support and the mothers who care for them are among America's poorest citizens, using these funds to provide an assured benefit is, at the very least, the compassionate thing to do. But it is also wise, because one-half of the next generation will be potentially eligible for child support.

THE DIFFERENCE BETWEEN THE ASSURED BENEFIT AND WELFARE

On occasion, I have heard some say that an assured child support benefit is just welfare by another name. It is true that both an assured benefit and welfare are public transfers. However, it is important to distinguish between public transfers that are income tested (like welfare) and those that are not (like Social Security).

The differences between what are conventionally called welfare programs, such as AFDC and food stamps, and universal programs, such as old-age insurance and the proposed assured child support benefit, are myriad. This is not just semantics. To say that the assured benefit is just welfare by another name because both are public transfers is to say that apples are just oranges by another name because apples and oranges are both fruit.

The assured benefit differs from AFDC in a myriad of ways. One must be poor to receive AFDC benefits. Because of this, as noted, AFDC contains strong disincentives to work and remarry; it isolates its beneficiaries from the social mainstream by funneling them through a separate bureaucracy that is expensive to administer; it stigmatizes them; and it provides no help whatsoever to the millions of single mothers and children who are economically insecure although not abjectly impoverished.

A universal assured child support benefit, on the other hand, is not for the poor alone but for children with nonresident parents from all income classes. Unlike with AFDC, eligibility for an assured child support benefit depends upon legal entitlement to private child support. And unlike with AFDC, an assured benefit would encourage poor mothers now mired within welfare to work and remarry. It would integrate these women and their children into the social mainstream. It would be very cheap to administer and would treat its beneficiaries with dignity. Finally, it would increase the economic security of all children who might be eligible for child support.

THE CSAS: AN ADDITION TO THE SOCIAL SECURITY MENU

A child support assurance system may be thought of as an addition to the American social security system. It is most analogous to survivors insurance. Like it, the CSAS aids children of all income classes who suffer an income loss due to the absence of a parent. Survivors' Insurance compensates for loss of income in the event of death; child support assurance compensates for loss of income arising from divorce, separation, and nonmarriage.

The percentage-of-income standard, in conjunction with routine income withholding, makes the financing of the CSAS similar to a proportional payroll tax, which is used to finance all American social insurance programs. In the case of the CSAS, however, the "tax" applies only to those who are legally liable for child support. This is the key difference between child support assurance and social insurance. With social insurance programs, contributions typically take place prior to the event requiring the insurance. With the CSAS, the nonresident parent pays child support only after moving out of the home. That is why its advocates in Wisconsin chose the name *assurance* rather than *insurance*.[9]

The assured benefit component of the CSAS makes the benefit structure of the system just like all of America's social insurance programs in that it provides greater benefits to low-income families than are justified on the basis of the families' contributions or taxes.[10]

Finally, a child support assurance system, like social security programs and the U.S. universal public school system, is designed to prevent poverty and welfare dependence. Remember that, despite the fact that the architects of the Social Security Act provided federal cash relief on an unprecedented scale and enacted three new permanent federal cash relief programs—aid to the aged, the blind, and dependent children—they remained uncomfortable with the widespread provision of cash relief, even for persons not expected to work. Even though poor widows and their children were already eligible for Aid to Dependent Children, the architects of the social security system advocated the creation of a survivors insurance program. Their strong preference for preventing, rather than relieving, poverty is evident in the following excerpt from the report of the 1938 Advisory Council on Social Security:

> While public assistance is now being provided to a large number of dependent children in this country on a needs-test basis, the arguments for substituting benefits as a matter of right in the case of children are even more convincing than in the case of aged persons. A democratic society has an immeasurable stake in avoiding the growth of a habit of dependence among its youth. The method of survivors' insurance not only sustains the concept that a child is supported through the efforts of the parent but affords a vital sense of security to the family unit.[11]

The CSAS, therefore, is based on the goals of the original architects of social insurance systems in the United States.

COSTS AND BENEFITS OF THE CSAS

The first question that policymakers ask about the CSAS is, How much will it cost? They also want to know how much it will reduce poverty and AFDC caseloads. In collaboration with several colleagues, I developed a microsimulation model to estimate the costs and benefits of the CSAS.[12]

Because of insufficient data, administrative costs are not considered in the estimates provided here. Routine establishment of paternity, regular updating of child support awards, and routine income withholding are all expected to lead to increases in administrative costs. To what extent these additional costs would be offset by reductions in current expenditures is difficult to say. The extra administrative costs of an assured child support benefit should be small once routine income withholding has become universal, because government agencies will be receiving and disbursing private child support payments to all eligible families. Except for the small minority of cases in which there would be no child support payment, the checks would have to be cut and the envelopes addressed even if there were no child support benefit. Only the amounts of the check would need to be changed.[13] These small extra costs of administering the assured benefit could easily be outweighed by the decrease in AFDC administrative costs that would result from decreases in caseloads.

The CSAS as a whole may increase or decrease costs because the increased costs of the assured benefit are offset by AFDC savings that arise principally from increased child support payments and secondarily from the improved work incentives of the CSAS. Table 3.1 presents estimates of costs (or savings) and reductions in poverty and AFDC caseloads for national child support assurance programs of different degrees of generosity and different degrees of effectiveness of child support collections.

Long-run costs and benefits.   The estimates in the top panel of Table 3.1 assume that collection of child support awards is 100 percent effective. That is, there are child support awards in all cases, that the awards are equal to the percentages described earlier, and that all the awards are paid in full.

The first row across in each section presents estimates in which there is no assured benefit. The next three rows give estimates in which the assured benefit level for the first child equals, respectively, $1,000, $2,000, and $3,000.[14] (Assured benefits for the second, third, fourth, fifth, and sixth child would be $1,000, $1,000, $500, $500, and $500, respectively, for all three levels of the assured benefit for the first child.)

Only the most generous assured benefit of $3,000 for the first child costs money. The savings for the less generous assured benefit levels arise because the extra dollars paid out for the assured benefit under the new system would be more than offset by increased child support collections and consequent reductions in welfare expenditures due to the fact that the child support and assured benefit money for women on AFDC is used to offset AFDC costs. In addition, AFDC costs are reduced by the increase in work and reductions in dependence on AFDC that the CSAS induces.

TABLE 3.1 / Estimated Benefits and Costs of a National Child Support Assurance System over Time, in 1985 Dollars

Assured Benefit Level	Reduction in Poverty Gap (%)	Reduction in AFDC Cases (%)	Net Cost (in Billions)
PERFECT SYSTEM			
0	24	20	-2.7
1,000	25	23	-2.5
2,000	30	33	-1.4
3,000	40	49	+0.7
SHORT RUN I[a]			
0	0	0	+0.0
1,000	2	3	+0.5
2,000	5	8	+2.1
3,000	9	14	+4.7
SHORT RUN II[b]			
0	2	2	-0.1
1,000	3	4	+0.1
2,000	5	8	+0.9
3,000	9	14	+2.7
INTERMEDIATE RUN[c]			
0	12	9	-1.1
1,000	13	12	-0.8
2,000	17	20	+0.1
3,000	24	32	+2.1

[a] No increase in child support award rates, award levels, or payment rates.
[b] Awards now set according to Wisconsin standard; no change in award rates or payment rates.
[c] Award rates and collection rates halfway between current levels and perfection; award levels equal to the Wisconsin standard.

The reductions in the poverty gap for families eligible for child support are substantial. The poverty gap is the difference between the income of a poor family and the income needed to bring the family up to the poverty line. Even with no assured benefit, increased child support collections would reduce the poverty gap by nearly one-quarter. Adding the assured benefit of $3,000 for the first child nearly doubles the reduction in poverty, from 24 percent to 40 percent. Similarly, reductions in welfare caseloads are very large, ranging from a low of 20 percent in the absence of an assured child support benefit to two and one-half times that amount, or 49 percent, with an assured benefit of $3,000.[15]

As I have already noted, the estimates in the top panel of Table 3.1 presume a perfect child support collection system. As of 1992, however, the collection system is a long way from perfection. Enactment of a child support assurance system would increase the proportion of cases with child support awards, the average level of awards, and the proportion of awards paid. What is not known now is by how much and how fast. Thus, the estimates in the top panel should be interpreted as lower bounds of the long-run costs and upper bounds of the long-run effects of the CSAS on reductions in poverty and welfare dependence.

Short-run costs and benefits. The second panel in Table 3.1 presents short-run, lower-bound estimates of the benefits and upper-bound estimates of the costs of the CSAS. The estimates are short-run in that they assume no increase in child support award rates, award levels, or payment rates. All three are expected to increase, so these assumptions underestimate benefits and overestimate costs.

The short-run benefits of the CSAS are quite modest. A $2,000 assured benefit reduces the poverty gap by only 5 percent and AFDC caseloads by only 8 percent. Even the assured benefit of $3,000 for the first child reduces the poverty gap by only 9 percent and AFDC caseloads by just 14 percent. These are not trivial effects. But they are only one-quarter of the upper-bound estimates of long-run benefits.

Furthermore, in the short run, with absolutely no improvements in child support enforcement, the CSAS would have positive net costs, ranging from $.5 billion to $4.7 billion. These net costs could be reduced substantially, and easily, by simply restricting eligibility to children whose awards have been updated to be in accordance with the Wisconsin percentage-of-income standard. If this single improvement in child support enforcement is achieved, as the results in the third panel of Table 3.1 indicate, the costs are reduced to virtually zero for a $1,000 assured benefit and to $.9 billion and $2.7 billion, respectively, for the $2,000 and

$3,000 assured benefit levels. It was awareness of these differences between the short- and long-run benefits and costs of the CSAS that led the architects of the Wisconsin CSAS to recommend to the state that it would be fiscally prudent to enact the program in stages, beginning with collection reforms. The country as a whole has already taken giant strides toward the CSAS on the collection side.

Finally, it is worth emphasizing that, so long as eligibility is limited to families with new or updated child support awards, even in the short run, the cost of a $1,000 assured child support benefit is practically zero. Thus, it is possible to enact a very small assured child support benefit and get started down the right path at practically no cost. Even the cost of a $2,000 assured benefit is less than $1 billion.

Intermediate-run costs and benefits.   The last panel in Table 3.1 presents some intermediate-run estimates of the benefits and costs of the CSAS. Both award rates and collection rates are halfway between their current levels and perfection. All award levels are assumed to be equal to the Wisconsin standard. The costs are small. An assured benefit of only $1,000 saves $.8 billion. The cost of an assured benefit of $2,000 is practically zero. Even an assured benefit of $3,000 costs only $2 billion.

Moreover, the intermediate-run benefits are fairly large. With an assured benefit of $2,000, both the poverty gap and the AFDC caseloads are reduced by almost 20 percent. With an assured benefit of $3,000, the poverty gap is reduced by 24 percent and the AFDC caseloads by 32 percent.

These estimates suggest that a new child support assurance system represents a marked improvement over the old child support system: It costs relatively little and yet achieves so much.

MOVEMENT TOWARD THE CSAS IN WISCONSIN AND NEW YORK

Initially, the CSAS had bipartisan support. Its principal advocates in the political world were Tom Loftus, a Democrat who became Majority Leader in the state assembly in 1981 and Speaker of the Assembly in 1983, and Donald Percy, who was Secretary of the

Wisconsin Department of Health and Social Services (DHSS) from 1977 to 1984. Percy was first appointed to office by Governor Martin Schreiber, a Democrat, and reappointed by Governor Lee Dreyfus, a Republican.

Between 1983 and 1987 Wisconsin moved in a series of gradual steps to statewide adoption of the essential features of the collection side of the CSAS: numerical standards for establishing a child support award and routine income withholding. In 1983 the Wisconsin legislature directed the Department of Health and Social Services to contract with ten counties routinely to withhold child support payment from the wages of all nonresident parents with new awards and publish a child support standard based on a percentage of the nonresident parent's income that judges and family court commissioners could use to determine child support obligations. The bill also contained a provision requiring all Wisconsin counties to adopt routine income withholding in all new cases as of July 1, 1987.

The standard was published by the DHSS and sent to all judges and family court commissioners in December 1983. It provided for a child support obligation equal to 17 percent for one child, and 25, 29, 31, and 34 percent, respectively, for two, three, four, and five or more children. Between January and May of 1984, ten counties had contracted with the DHSS to test the use of immediate income assignments in a pilot program.

The 1985 Wisconsin budget bill contained new child support legislation that permitted additional counties to begin immediate withholding prior to July 1, 1987, and made the DHSS percentage-of-income standard the presumptive child support award as of that month. This meant that awards could depart from the standard only if the judge justified such action in writing. Finally, the 1985 bill gave the DHSS authority, subject to final approval by the Joint Finance Committee, to implement the assured benefit on a demonstration basis in several counties.

Soon after the 1985 legislation was enacted, nearly twenty additional counties began implementing routine income withholding. Milwaukee, the largest county in the state, began withholding in January 1986. By July 1, 1987, all but two or three of Wisconsin's seventy-two counties had implemented routine income withholding.

Meanwhile, state officials also successfully sought federal legislation to allow Wisconsin to use federal funds to help finance the state's assured child support benefit. Because the assured benefit would reduce AFDC costs, of which the federal government pays about half, it agreed to allow Wisconsin to use the resulting savings to help finance the assured benefit. The agreement, contained in the Child Support Enforcement Amendments of 1984, extends for seven years: from the last quarter of 1986 through 1993.[16]

As of 1990, only Wisconsin and New York were authorized to use federal funds that would otherwise have been devoted to AFDC to help pay for an assured child support benefit. Implementation of the assured benefit was delayed in Wisconsin by political disagreements, first within Governor Anthony Earl's administration (1983–1986) and then within Governor Tommy Thompson's administration (1987–1990 and 1991–1994). As of 1992, the state had yet to institute a pilot program, and it seems unlikely that the assured benefit will be tested there. (As will be discussed in chapter 6, a very limited version is being tried in New York.)

LESSONS OF THE WISCONSIN EXPERIENCE

Early data on the extent to which the Wisconsin courts really used the standard after it became the presumptive obligation in July 1987 indicate that, though it is increasingly used to establish the initial child support order, in most cases, this order is not expressed as a percentage of income.[17] Rather, the percentages in the standard are used to establish a fixed dollar amount for the child support order. Because the incomes of nonresident parents, on average, increase over time and because the low level of child support orders is attributable in part to the inability of courts to regularly update awards to take account of changes in income, the failure to express orders as a percentage of income is very serious.

Based on data from the original ten county pilot programs, it appears that routine withholding within these counties was not universally implemented.[18] Nearly 80 percent of the nonresident parents had income from which a child support obligation could be withheld, but it was actually withheld from only about 40 percent in 1984 and 60 percent by 1986. The Wisconsin experience has demonstrated the need to persevere in the effort to improve collections. This takes time and involves many changes over a long period. No single change in the law can do the job alone.

REMAINING ISSUES

The CSAS may be viewed as a three-legged stool, in which each element—the award standard, withholding, and the assured benefit—is as vital to its balance as the other two. The nation has already taken great strides toward the adoption of the two key collection features of a child support assurance system. The Family Support Act of 1988 requires all states to adopt numerical standards for establishing child support awards, to update awards at least every third year, and to withhold child support obligations from wages and other sources of income in all cases. Although many collection-side issues remain, as will be discussed in the next two chapters, the CSAS now has two, albeit wobbly, legs to stand on. It is essential to its success that the assured benefit also be adopted, for that is what creates the delicate balance of incentives that will make the CSAS work. Designed correctly, this benefit can reduce economic insecurity and welfare dependence, foster the establishment of paternity, and provide the incentive for strong government enforcement. It would improve the functioning of the other two elements and the CSAS as a whole.

NOTES

1. Specifically, the request came from Michael Barth, director of the division of Income Security Policy/Analysis in the office of the Assistant Secretary for Planning and Evaluation of the federal Department of Health, Education and Welfare.
2. Isabel V. Sawhill, "Developing Normative Standards for Child Support and Alimony Payments," Working Paper 992-04, The Urban Institute, Washington, D.C., September 1977.
3. Family Support Act of 1988, Public Law No. 100-485 103, 102 Stat. 2343, 2346, codified as 42 USC 667 (b)(2), effective October 14, 1989, provides "There shall be a rebuttable presumption, in any judicial or administrative proceeding for the award of child sup-

port, that the amount of the award which would result from the application of such guidelines is the correct amount of child support to be awarded. A written finding or specific finding on the record that the application of the guidelines would be unjust or inappropriate in a particular case, as determined under criteria established by the State, shall be sufficient to rebut the presumption in that case."

4. Garfinkel and Klawitter, "Effects of Routine Income Withholding," pp. 155–177.

5. Jacques Van der Gaag, "On Measuring the Costs of Children," in *Child Support: Weakness of the Old and Features of a Proposed New System*, edited by Irwin Garfinkel and Marygold S. Melli, Vol. 1, Institute for Research on Poverty Special Report #32A, Madison, Wis.: University of Wisconsin-Madison, 1982, p. 21.

6. Isabel Sawhill "Discrimination and Poverty among Women Who Head Families," *Signs*, Vol. 2, No. 3, 1976, pp. 201–211. For a more recent discussion, Charles Michaelopolis and Irwin Garfinkel, "Reducing Welfare Dependence and Poverty via Earnings and Child Support: Wishful Thinking or Realistic Possibility?" Institute for Research on Poverty Discussion Paper #882-89, University of Wisconsin-Madison, 1989.

7. Michaelopolis and Garfinkel, "Reducing Welfare Dependence and Poverty."

8. Of course, there are a variety of other methods by which AFDC savings could be directed to poor children. For example, they could be used to increase AFDC benefits or to fund child care or training for AFDC beneficiaries. But, although increases in these areas are desirable, only a benefit conditional upon the establishment of paternity leads to increases in paternity establishment. See appendix 1.A for a description of child support set-asides within welfare and a comparison of this alternative to an assured child support benefit.

9. Sarah Harder, a linguist from the University of Wisconsin at Eau Claire and a member of the state advisory committee on child support reform created by the Wisconsin Department of Health and Social Services, chose the name and convinced the advisory committee of its correctness.

10. In the U.S. social insurance system two benefit provisions favor low-income workers: progressive replacement rates and minimum benefits. Benefits are equal to a fraction of previous earnings. Replacement rates are progressive because, the lower the previous earnings, the higher the fraction.

11. *Final Report of the 1937–38 Advisory Council on Social Security*, in 50th anniversary edition of *The Report of the Committee on Economic Security of 1935*, Washington, D.C.: National Conference on Social Welfare, 1985, pp. 192–193.

12. For a description of the microsimulation model used to derive these estimates, see Irwin Garfinkel, Philip K. Robins, Patrick Wong, and Daniel Meyer, "The Wisconsin Child Support Assurance System: Estimated Effects on Poverty, Labor Supply, Caseloads, and Costs," *Journal of Human Resources*, Vol. 25, 1990, pp. 1–31.

13. The major additional cost of administering the assured benefit arises from the need to keep account of assured benefit disbursements from month to month. For example, a nonresident parent may pay more child support during the course of the year than the assured benefit but slip below the level of the assured benefit for one month. In this case, the child support check in that month should equal the assured benefit level, but the check in a subsequent month (or months) should be reduced, to assure that, on an annual basis, there is no public subsidy. Alternatively, this could be handled via income tax returns at the end of the year.

14. The public-subsidy portion of the assured benefit is taxable income for the resident parent, and the federal revenue derived from making it taxable is subtracted from the estimated costs of the assured benefit.

15. The estimates of welfare caseload reductions may be too high or too low, because they are based on annual data, whereas eligibility is based on monthly income.

16. In effect, Wisconsin was given a block grant to run both a child support assurance system and the AFDC system at the same cost to the federal government as the old AFDC system alone. Extra costs or savings are solely to be borne by or be of benefit to the state.

17. Irwin Garfinkel and Judith Bartfeld, "Utilization of the Percentage-of-Income Standard: A Preliminary Report," Report to the Department of Health and Human Services, State of Wisconsin, 1991.

18. Garfinkel and Klawitter, "Effects of Routine Income Withholding," pp. 155–177.

4 / Feasibility of Increasing Child Support Payments

In chapter 3, I showed that, if child support collections increase sufficiently, a Child Support Assurance System that reduces the poverty gap and AFDC recipients by nearly one-fifth could be cost neutral. In this chapter I ask whether such an increase in child support collections is feasible. The answer in brief is yes. But achieving sufficient increases in child support collections to make the CSAS cost neutral will take time and will require further legislation, as well as effective implementation of existing legislation and increased investments in child support enforcement.

The chapter begins with an explanation of the need to improve all features of child support enforcement, in order to achieve appreciable gains in total payments. The next several sections review each of the features that must be improved and appraise the short- and long-run prospects for success. The last two sections put the pieces together again, in order to assess overall performance in the recent past and overall prospects for the future.

IMPROVING ENFORCEMENT

All features of enforcement must be improved. Total child support payments depend upon three elements: (1) the proportion of children potentially eligible for support who actually have child support awards, (2) the level of child support awards, and (3) the proportion of awards that are actually paid. All three elements are critical.

As of 1992, all three elements are low. Only 60 percent of those potentially eligible for child support have awards. Existing awards are equal to only about one-half to two-thirds the level of awards prescribed by either the income shares or the Wisconsin percentage-of-income standard.[1] And, on average, those with awards pay only about 59 percent of the amount they owe.[2] I estimate that getting awards in all cases without improving either the level of awards or the proportion paid would increase child support collections in the United States by $4.4 billion. Increasing the level of awards to those prescribed in Wisconsin's percentage-of-income standard without increasing the proportion with awards or the percentage paid would increase child support collections by $6.5 billion. Increasing the proportion paid to 100 percent of what is owed without increasing the proportion with awards or the level of awards would increase payments by $2.9 billion.[3]

These estimates are useful for putting various reforms of the child support enforcement system into proper perspective. For example, the single reform that has gotten the most media attention is routine income withholding. Withholding child support obligations from wages and other sources of income on a routine basis would increase the ratio of child support paid to child support owed. Yet the estimates just mentioned indicate that, by itself, increasing the payment rate has the least potential for increasing child support payments.

Even more important, the estimates indicate the need to improve all aspects of the system at once. If there were child support awards in all cases, all the awards were reasonable, and all that was owed were paid, child support payments in the United States would increase by $25.6 billion. This is nearly twice the sum of the improvements resulting from perfecting each element by itself. Here is a case in which the whole is greater than the sum of its parts. An improvement in any element makes an improvement in any other element more efficacious.

GETTING CHILD SUPPORT AWARDS: THE CRUCIAL FIRST STEP

If the legal obligation to pay child support is not established, the chances that it will be paid are substantially diminished.[4] The crucial first step in securing payment of child support from non-resident parents, then, is to establish their legal liability to pay. Over 80 percent of divorced women and nearly 50 percent of separated women have child support awards, whereas less than 20 percent of never-married women have them.[5] The main reason for this low rate among never-married mothers is that establishing the paternity of children born out of wedlock is so problematic. I start this analysis, therefore, with a prognosis for improvement in establishing paternity.

Unwed Parents and Paternity Establishment

Establishing the legal liability to pay child support is more difficult if the parents are not married, because of the requirement that paternity be established to obtain a child support award. Because there is such a poor rate of establishing paternity and securing child support awards for children born out of wedlock, many individuals believe that there must be severe limits to how much improvement can be made. For instance, I am frequently asked, Isn't there a large proportion of unwed mothers who don't know who the fathers of their children are or at least don't know where they are? Isn't it inordinately expensive to track down and get blood tests from potential fathers who, once found, are unlikely to be able to pay much child support? And, isn't there a danger of interfering with the rights of mothers to privacy? Let's examine the answers and their implications.

Locating the Fathers

There are *not* a lot of unwed mothers who don't know who the fathers of their children are. For a mother to be ignorant of the identity of her child's father, she'd have to be rather promiscuous. But, very few women have more than one sexual partner at a time.[6] Among never-married mothers without child support awards in the Current Population Survey-Child Support Supplement (CPS-CSS), only 6 percent said the reason they did not have one was that they were unable to establish paternity.[7] And, as there are other reasons aside from not knowing who the father is for being unable to establish paternity, 6 percent is almost certainly an upper-bound estimate of the women who fall into this category. (Other reasons include cases of rape or incest, cases where the father lives in another state, and cases where child support enforcement officials think paternity is not worth pursuing because they think the father cannot pay.)

Although it is rare for unwed mothers not to know who the fathers of their children are, it is quite common for them to report that they do not know *where* the fathers are. Fully one-third of never-married mothers without child support awards in the CPS-CSS survey indicated that they would like to have an award but were unable to locate the fathers. Furthermore, child support enforcement officials in large cities report that they fail to pursue a large proportion of paternity cases because of their inability to locate putative fathers.[8]

Despite the CPS-CSS data and the experience of child support enforcement officials, there are two reasons for believing that, in a large proportion of the cases where failure to locate explains the absence of an award, unwed mothers could help locate the fathers. First, the mother's knowledge of the whereabouts of the father is clearly a matter of timing. At the time of conception, certainly, most mothers know where to find the father-to-be. Indeed, during pregnancy and even soon after birth, the majority of mothers probably know the whereabouts of the father. Of course, as the length of time between pregnancy and the attempt to locate the father increases, so increases the number of mothers who have stopped seeing the fathers of their children and who, therefore, may not know how to contact them.

Second, by claiming not to know the whereabouts of the putative father, mothers who wish to receive welfare can protect the identity of the father and still satisfy the federal requirement that mothers on AFDC cooperate with child support enforcement officials. Because the courts have ruled that welfare benefits cannot be denied unless there is very strong evidence of failure to cooperate, if a mother says she doesn't know where the father lives, it is quite expensive, and perhaps even impossible, to prove that she is lying. Thus, the costs of falsely claiming not to know the whereabouts of the father are low. In contrast, the benefits to the mother may be high. By protecting the father, she may avoid his ill will or, more positively, curry his favor, continue the relationship, and, even possibly, receive informal, unreported, child support from him. Consequently, it seems reasonable to conclude that some unwed mothers falsely claim not to know the whereabouts of the fathers of their children.

These two considerations imply that, if efforts to establish paternity began earlier and if the incentives for mothers to cooperate were improved, it is likely that the location of fathers would be less problematic. Thus, the prognosis for improvement in this area hinges on the extent to which paternity-establishment efforts can begin earlier and to which incentives for cooperation can be improved.

Costs of Establishing Paternity

Establishing paternity and securing child support awards for children born out of wedlock is more costly than securing them for children of dissolved marital unions. Furthermore, on average, unwed fathers have lower incomes than divorced and separated nonresident parents, and, as a consequence, they can afford to pay less child support. Thus, it is easy to see why child support enforcement agencies that are short of staff give the lowest priority to pursuing child support for children born out of wedlock.

The fact that the benefit–cost ratio of child support enforcement is lower for children born out of wedlock than for children from dissolved marital unions does not mean that the costs of establishing paternity and securing child support awards *exceed* the benefits. Indeed, the one study done on the matter indicates that, within three to four years, the benefits of establishing paternity and securing support exceed the costs.[9] Furthermore, the costs of establishing paternity are likely to decrease as states follow the federal recommendation to establish expedited civil procedures for this. Similarly, the costs of locating fathers are likely to drop substantially and the proportion of contested cases is likely to decrease if paternity establishment is begun routinely at birth or during pregnancy.

A Woman's Right to Privacy

Will stronger efforts to establish paternity conflict with women's rights to privacy? If an unwed mother is not interested in pursuing paternity, to what extent should the state compel her to do so? Some would argue that the decision should be the mother's alone and is none of the state's business. Others are more concerned with current practices that subject welfare mothers to very personal questions about their sexual behavior. The importance of the privacy issue is highlighted by the large amount of unwed mothers without awards (45 percent) who report in the CPS-CSS that the reason they do not have a child support award is that they do not want one.

Anyone who has read the forms that unwed welfare mothers are required to fill out as part of the paternity-establishment procedure would find it difficult to deny that this procedure is invasive. In large part, the detailed questions about the mother's sexual history are driven by the concern to be able to prove in court that the putative father is the father. It is likely that, if paternity establishment were commenced routinely during pregnancy or soon after birth, much of this invasiveness could be avoided because fathers would probably be more cooperative.

Even in cases where no public support is involved, the mother's decision with respect to paternity establishment is not strictly private. The child also has a stake in the decision, and the child's interests may not always coincide with the mother's interests. At some point in the child's life, for example, knowledge of the father's genetic and health history may be of great importance. Still, because of the presumption that, in most cases, the mother is the best judge of the child's interests, to justify public intervention when no public funding is involved requires a demonstration that the potential benefits of public intervention are great.

In cases where the mother seeks public assistance for her child, her decision about whether to attempt to establish paternity and secure a child support award has financial implications for taxpayers. Thus, in this case, there is no merit to the argument that this decision is strictly a private matter. Moreover, there is no presumption that the mother is the best judge of the taxpayers' interest. It is reasonable for taxpayers, who support the child, to insist that, in return for their support, the mother cooperate in attempts to get the father of the child to bear his fair share. After thorough debate in the early 1970s, this is what the U.S. Congress concluded.[10] Unless mothers have good cause for avoiding paternity establishment such as rape, incest, or the threat of physical or emotional harm to them or their children, they must cooperate in seeking to establish paternity.

Although the cooperation requirement can be justified, it has been noted that it can easily be avoided and, therefore, has not proved to be sufficient. In this context, the assured child support benefit takes on added importance. So long as eligibility for the assured benefit depends upon the existence of a child support award, for which paternity establishment is a precondition, the assured benefit creates a potentially powerful incentive for mothers to help identify and locate the fathers of their children.

Reasons to Expect Improvement in Establishing Paternity

Despite the very poor record, and all of the difficulties associated with improving it, there are good reasons for believing that eventually it will be possible to establish paternity in the majority of cases of out-of-wedlock birth. Sweden, which has an out-of-wedlock birthrate that rivals that of the United States, has been establishing paternity in over 90 percent of out-of-wedlock births since the end of World War II.[11] Of course, there are some telling differences between the two countries. Because of its small size and its equivalent of an identity card, it is virtually impossible to disappear in Sweden. Furthermore, a large proportion of the parents of Swedish children born out of wedlock are living together. Yet U.S. experience suggests that we can do substantially better. Whereas the United States as a whole establishes paternity in less than 30 percent of out-of-wedlock births, the state of Michigan establishes paternity in about two-thirds of such cases. Texas, on the other hand, establishes paternity in only 2 percent of them.[12] There is nothing mysterious about Michigan's relatively successful record, because it is more committed to enforcing child support. Michigan has some of the oldest and the strongest child support enforcement laws in the country and spends a great deal more per potentially eligible child than does Texas. (Expenditures in 1988 per child for enforcement in Michigan and Texas were $106 and $38, respectively.)

In response to incentives and prodding from the federal government, states are doing much better in establishing paternity than they did only as long ago as the late 1970s. The proportion of paternities established in out-of-wedlock births increased between 1979 and 1985 from 19 percent to 28 percent.[13] Furthermore, there is good reason to believe that there will be substantial improvements in the 1990s. The 1988 Family Support Act contained by far the strongest federal legislation to date for establishing paternity. Recall that the legislation includes a requirement that (1) states obtain the social security numbers of both parents in conjunction with the issuance of birth certificates, (2) states either establish paternity in at least half the cases or increase the proportion of cases in which they establish paternity by three percentage points each year, and (3) there be federal funding of 90 percent of the costs of blood tests.

Requiring states to obtain social security numbers in conjunction with the issuance of birth certificates not only provides them with useful information they can use later to help establish paternity but, more important, also nudges them in the correct direction of seeking to establish paternity as early as possible. The requirement that states currently having weak records increase the proportion of cases in which they establish paternity will almost certainly lead to improvements. The federal funding of blood tests removes a financial barrier to state action.

Because Michigan already establishes paternity in about two-thirds of out-of-wedlock births and because the Family Support Act of 1988 can be expected to lead to substantial improvements in paternity establishment in most states, I think it reasonable to expect that, by the turn of the century, the country as a whole will be establishing paternity in about half of all out-of-wedlock births. But that would still leave much to be done to reach the ideal. In cities and neighborhoods in which establishing paternity remained the exception rather than the rule, the cost of increasing paternity establishment would continue to be relatively high. Every nonresident father knows that most fathers do not get saddled with paternity and consequent child support obligations. This knowledge encourages them to resist being identified. Word gets around of how mothers can satisfy the welfare department requirement for cooperation and at the same time protect their children's fathers, so that, at the very least, location expenses are incurred. In addition, if the putative father is located and denies paternity, blood tests are necessary.

Progress requires establishment of paternity closer to conception, preferably no later than right after birth, and rewarding of mothers in the form of assured child support benefits for establishing paternity. Both of these investments in paternity establishment will increase costs in the short run, but, in the long run, it is possible that enforcement costs will actually decrease.

Imagine the following state of affairs. Paternity is established as a matter of course by a public health official immediately after birth. The officials inform the new mother of all the benefits of establishing paternity, including an assured child support benefit. They then seek the identity of the putative father from the mother, contact him, enable him to establish his paternity, and get him involved with the child. This is similar to the Swedish system that works so well. The state of Washington has begun to implement such a system, and officials report large increases in paternity establishment. If in the near future, we enact an assured child support benefit and routinely establish paternity at the time of birth, it does not seem unduly optimistic to imagine that, by the end of the first quarter of the twenty-first century, the United States will have established paternity respectfully and inexpensively in the vast majority of cases.

INCREASING THE PROPORTION OF SEPARATED WOMEN WITH AWARDS

To some extent, mothers who are separated are in a transitional state on their way to divorce. This helps to explain the smaller proportion of separated mothers than divorced mothers who have child support awards. Whereas only 43 percent of separated mothers have child support awards, another 14 percent do not have

awards because their final divorce agreements are pending.[14] Even
assuming that all of the 14 percent will get awards, that still leaves
43 percent without child support awards, compared with less than
20 percent of the divorced. (In addition, some portion of the separated will reconcile at some point.)

Of those without awards, about a quarter did not want them.
Of those who did not have an award but wanted one, most reported that they did not have one because of inability to locate
the father. As was the case with unwed mothers, some portion
of separated mothers who report that they do not know the location of their former spouses are doing so to fulfill the welfare
requirement to cooperate in seeking child support.

Some separated mothers do not want an award because they
know that their former spouses have never earned much in the
past and are not likely to earn much in the future. (This includes
a portion of the quarter without awards who say they do not want
them, plus a portion of the much larger group who report that
they do not know the whereabouts of their former spouses.) The
prospect of receiving an assured child support benefit if they secure a child support award would undoubtedly induce some of
these mothers to seek awards.

On the other hand, a good portion of separated mothers are
unable to locate their former mates. Unlike in the case of out-of-
wedlock births, there are no grounds for believing that simply
starting the location process earlier would solve most of the problem. For separated mothers, there is no natural intervention point
like a health examination during pregnancy or the birth of the
child, which normally occurs before the father disappears. Separated mothers may not seek help until their spouses have left,
and, by then, contact has often already ceased. How much improvement in location practices can be expected in the foreseeable
future is not clear. Current efforts to locate nonresident parents
are time-intensive individual investigations. Some improvement
should result from automation of records, because computer
searches of records are cheap. But, in many cases, the best sources
of location are relatives and friends of the nonresident parent.
Similarly, improvements in interstate child support enforcement
practices should facilitate improvements in locating fathers. Finally, there should be some improvement over time as enforce-

ment officials learn from experience. It is impossible to say how great these improvements might be but what is clear is that the process of change will be slow and painstaking.

INCREASING THE PROPORTION OF DIVORCED WOMEN WITH AWARDS

As of 1985, 82 percent of divorced and remarried mothers had child support awards. Less than 1 percent indicated that the reason for not having an award was that their final divorce decree was still pending. Another 2 percent indicated that they had a property settlement or joint custody in lieu of a child support award. Thus, the absence of awards in this group is a problem in only about 15 percent of the cases. Among those without awards or substitutes for awards, about half indicated that they did not want a child support award, and the other half indicated that they wanted an award but could not get one, principally because they couldn't locate the father.[15] There are two reasons for expecting improvements: first, better location efforts through computerization, better interstate enforcement practices, and better knowledge from experience; second, an assured child support benefit increasing incentives for divorced mothers to seek awards.

THE PROGNOSIS FOR INCREASING THE LEVEL OF AWARDS

The requirement that states use numerical guidelines for establishing and maintaining adequate levels of child support should lead to substantial increases in the amount of child support awards. All but a few states have adopted numerical guidelines similar to those of Wisconsin or Colorado. If these guidelines had been used to determine all current awards, and if all awards had been kept up to date, child support obligations in 1985 would have totaled between $16.7 and $19.6 billion, rather than the actual amount of $9.7 billion.[16]

A very early study of the effect of guidelines in Colorado, Hawaii, and Illinois indicated that they led to an increase of 15 percent in the average level of initial child support awards.[17] This finding is very encouraging when one considers that the increase only refers to initial awards and, therefore, omits gains from updating old awards; that the 15 percent increase reflects changes in the first year after enactment of the guidelines; that there is substantial evidence of departure from the guidelines; and that legal change takes time to occur.

On the other hand, the gap between the 15 percent increase in this early implementation study and the 70 percent to 100 percent increase predicted by microsimulation models calls attention to all the uncertainties of the effects of guidelines on child support award levels. Because courts are permitted to depart from guidelines when the outcome is deemed to be unfair to any of the parties, it is possible that this loophole will be used to undermine the intent of the law.

Equally important, there may be a great deal of slippage in updating child support awards. The new federal law requires states to review awards every three years, but the review need not lead to updating. Moreover, updating every third year, rather than annually, is expected to reduce average award levels by about 5 percent.[18] An even more serious concern is that, as yet, the updating applies only to cases handled by state offices of child support, and they are, therefore, mostly AFDC cases. Whether this provision will be extended to all child support cases depends upon future legislation. On the other hand, it is possible that all child support cases will become IV-D cases. Some states have already made this so. The universality of routine withholding also pushes all the states in this direction.

Perhaps the most serious concern is that the courts will find the updating so burdensome and costly that they will find a cheap method of review that avoids updating in the vast majority of cases. In the past, laws made it very difficult to revise child support awards in order to avoid overburdening the courts.[19] How burdensome and costly it will be to update child support awards will depend in large measure on the complexity of the numerical guidelines and the extent to which updating procedures can be handled administratively. (The importance of simplicity is discussed in detail in chapter 5.) Under the best of circumstances some administrative costs will be associated with updating. At this point, we have no way of knowing whether these costs will be sufficient in many jurisdictions to deter the effort.

Finally, and perhaps the most important point, there may be a legislative reversal in the priority given to enforcing child support. Already, at least two legal scholars, Harry D. Krause and David L. Chambers, who helped strengthen child support enforcement in the past, have suggested that the United States has now gone too far. Krause argued that the new strictness of child support enforcement was inconsistent with the new laxness in sexual conduct and suggested that the former be brought in line with the latter. Chambers called for terminating all child support responsibilities after a few years.[20] Such proposals remind us that the current enthusiasm for enforcing child support might diminish and even reverse. More than that, they remind us that whether child support enforcement will continue to improve or not is largely a matter of political choice.

In short, guidelines will lead to large increases in child support award levels over time, if they are actually implemented and not undermined by judicial discretion; if they are used to update, as well as set, initial awards; if they are used for both setting and updating initial awards for the nonwelfare and the welfare population; and if they are not eviscerated by reversals in the public commitment to enforce the parental child support obligation. On balance, there is good reason to believe that the new child support standards and updating of awards required by the 1988 Family Support Act will substantially increase the average level of child support awards, but previous differences between law on the books and law in practice suggests that it is very important to monitor the implementation of the child support guidelines.

THE PROGNOSIS FOR INCREASING THE PROPORTION OF AWARDS COLLECTED

Recall that fathers who have legal obligations to pay child support currently pay 59 percent of their obligations, about half of the nonresident parents paying the full amount owed, another quarter paying part, and the last quarter paying nothing. The principal reasons for believing that we can improve upon this record are (1) the requirement in the 1988 Family Support Act that all states adopt routine income withholding laws, and (2) the increasing computerization of child support enforcement. Routine withholding alone, as suggested, would increase the national amount of child support collections out of total child support obligations from 59 percent to between 65 percent and 77 percent. Such an increase is certainly impressive. Furthermore, it should be reinforced by computerization and better interstate enforcement.

Since 1980, the federal government has offered to pay 90 percent of the costs that states incur to develop modern computerized record systems for their child support enforcement systems. It has taken the states an inordinately long time to computerize for several reasons including the lack of cooperation between the administrative and judicial branches of government and between state and local government agencies. Most states, however, are now well on their way. The importance of computerization cannot be overstressed. The number of parents who owe child support is so large that to attempt to keep track of them one by one with paper files is an overwhelming task.

During the early 1980s I visited a child support enforcement office in a Wisconsin county. I have a lasting visual impression of the office: five or six worktables completely covered with stacks of child support enforcement files. Wisconsin then had a law requiring child support enforcement officials to withhold child support payments from wages if the nonresident parent fell one month behind. The official I met with explained that his office lacked sufficient staff to implement the law. He guessed that cases were usually four or five months delinquent before withholding was implemented. The stacks of child support files that covered every inch of the worktables in his office provided evidence of an outmoded system that had been overwhelmed by the law of large numbers.

Once records are computerized, this problem will be alleviated. The computer can be programmed to check for and respond to delinquencies (for instance, by writing letters of inquiry to nonresident parents and their employers). Computers can also be programmed to check other data sources, such as social security payroll records, to find out if the nonresident parent has obtained a new job. Most important of all, computers are time- and cost-efficient.

Converting from a manual to a computerized management system is costly, however. The computers themselves are expensive, but more costly is the development of software to run them. Fortunately, as noted, the federal government has offered to pay 90 percent of the costs of this investment, wisely betting this will pay off in the form of increased child support collections.

Finally, improvements in interstate child support enforcement would also lead to improvements in collection. Interstate enforcement is important because estimates suggest that, in about 30 percent of all child support cases, the nonresident parent lives in a different state from his child.[21] (It is also worth noting that improvement in interstate enforcement could lead to improvement in award rates and levels, as well as in payment levels.) At this point the commission appointed by Congress to make recommendations for strengthening interstate enforcement has not made its report, so it is too early to ascertain whether there will be any real improvements in this area.

Although routine income withholding, computerization, and, perhaps, improvements in interstate child support enforcement will lead to increases in the proportion of child support obligations that are actually paid, there are two improvements in other dimensions of the system that are likely to lead to decreases in the proportion paid. First, as the proportion of children potentially eligible for support who actually get awards increases, the proportion of nonresident parents who work irregularly will increase. For example, as noted, fathers of children born out of wedlock are, on average, more likely to work irregularly than divorced fathers. It is more difficult to collect child support from irregular than steadily employed workers. Thus, we can expect that the ratio of child support paid to child support owed will be lower for the new cases brought into the system. Second, as child support awards increase, the incentive for avoidance will increase. How much more avoidance will result is impossible to say. Similarly, it is impossible to say at this point how much worse the payment ratios of the new recruits to the child support system will be. What is clear, however, is that increases in the proportion of cases with awards and the level of awards will tend to reduce the pay-to-owe ratio. That the average pay-to-owe ratio can actually decrease as a result of progress in other dimensions of the child support enforcement system indicates that partial measures do not give the clearest picture of overall progress.

THE OVERALL RECORD TO DATE

The child support provisions of the Family Support Act of 1988 represent the culmination of a fifteen-year trend toward stronger enforcement of child support obligations. There should, therefore, already be some evidence of the efficacy of our efforts.

There are two sources of national data on child support collections over time. The first, the Current Population Survey-Child Support Supplement, is a nationally representative sample of mothers with children potentially eligible for child support. As described, this survey has been conducted every other year since 1979. The second source is annual reports by the federal office of child support enforcement that compile data from state offices on annual child support collections.

The federal reports include information collected by state agencies on behalf of children both on welfare and not on welfare. Although the data on collections for both classifications of children show a huge increase over time, we focus on only that for children on AFDC, because the data on collections for non-AFDC cases are not a reliable guide to improvements in collections.

Reported collections have increased over time in part because states report more of what is being collected. They are required to report on child support collection for all welfare and other families to which they provided services. In 1978, the states provided services to only a very small proportion of nonwelfare families. Slowly but surely, they are serving an increasing proportion of them. Some of these families would have received at least some child support in the absence of the service; yet these payments would not be counted unless the service were provided. This is not true for AFDC cases, because the states both have a financial incentive and are required to report all child support collections for AFDC cases.

Between 1976 and 1988 child support collections for AFDC cases increased eightfold, from $.2 billion to $1.5 billion. These raw numbers paint an overoptimistic picture. Collections for AFDC cases went up in part because of an increase in the number of AFDC cases and in part because there was significant inflation between 1976 and 1988. To abstract from these limitations in the raw data, I calculated the average child support collection per AFDC case in 1988 dollars for both 1976 and 1988. The figures are, respectively, $118 and $398. Although this increase is much smaller than that for the raw data, it is nevertheless huge. It represents an average annual increase in collections of 28 percent.

Comparing increases in collections to increases in costs of collections also paints a positive picture. Between 1983 and 1988, collections for AFDC cases grew by about $.5 billion, whereas the total costs of collections grew by slightly less than $.2 billion.[22] On the other hand, because the federal government pays for the bulk of child support enforcement expenditures and the states and recipients get the bulk of collections, in recent years the federal government has been losing money on child support enforcement.[23] It can only be hoped that this will not lead to pressures in Congress to cut back on the federal role in child support enforcement.

The picture conveyed by the Current Population Survey-Child Support Supplement data is more mixed. There is evidence of some progress between 1978 and 1987. The proportion of those potentially eligible for child support and legally entitled to receive it grew by three percentage points, and the proportion of child support owed that was paid grew by four percentage points. On the other hand, average child support payments in 1987 dollars fell from $2,248 to $2,063. The source of this decline must be a decline in the real value of child support awards, because we know that the proportion of awards being paid increased between 1978 and 1987.

The average real value of child support awards decreased between 1978 and 1987 from $3,371 to $3,017. (Note that, in each survey, all women with children under 21 who were potentially eligible for child support were interviewed. Thus, in each survey, the child support awards had been made between one and twenty years earlier.) Recent research provides us with some understanding of the causes of this decline.[24] First, a good deal of the decline in real awards was due to the failure to update.[25] But the most important factor in accounting for the decline appears to be the increase in the ratio of resident parents' earnings to nonresident parents' earnings.[26] Awards have declined because many courts consider the incomes of both resident and nonresident parents in establishing child support and because the ratio of women's to men's annual earnings increased dramatically during the 1970s and 1980s. (Although the ratio of women's to men's hourly earnings remained relatively constant between 1960 and 1980, increasing somewhat during the 1980s, the ratio of women's to men's annual earnings increased dramatically because of the great increase in the number of hours worked by women.) Also, the composition of those eligible for child support awards has changed over time, so that paternity cases make up a larger proportion of the total. The proportion of women potentially eligible for child support who were never married increased from 20 percent in 1981 to 28 percent in 1987.[27] On average, fathers of children born out of wedlock are much poorer than divorced fathers.

Two provisions of the Family Support Act of 1988 address the first two reasons for declining awards. The numerical guidelines adopted by the states will increase initial child support awards even in families where residing parents have substantial earnings. And child support awards in cases handled by state offices of child support must now be examined for updating at least every three years. The third reason for declining awards, a shift in the types of families with awards, is a sign of progress rather than a problem, because it shows that more never-married mothers are getting awards.

The importance of reversing the decline in the real value of child support awards cannot be exaggerated. Recent research indicates that the decline in award levels more than offset all the other improvements in the child support system between 1978 and 1985.[28] Given its importance in accounting for the lack of overall progress in child support enforcement, it is worth repeating our highly qualified summary judgment about the prognosis for increasing award levels in the future. Guidelines will lead to large increases in child support award levels over time if they are

- Actually implemented and not undermined by judicial discretion
- Used to update, as well as set, initial awards
- Used for setting initial awards and updating for the nonwelfare, as well as the welfare, population
- Not eviscerated by reversals in public commitment to enforce the parental child support obligation

At first glance, the pictures painted by the survey data and the office of child support data appear to differ substantially, but they are actually quite consistent. The Office of Child Support Enforcement (OCSE) data focus on child support enforcement for children on welfare. The CPS-CSS data cover the entire population. If one looks at the latter data to compare improvements in child support enforcement for poor children with those for all children eligible for child support, one finds that improvements in child support enforcement were much greater among poor children than among all eligible children as a whole. Whereas the percentage of potentially eligible women with child support awards increased between 1978 and 1987 from 48.3 percent to 51.3 percent, the percentage of poor women with awards increased from 30.2 percent to 38.6 percent. Similarly, payment rates increased from 71.7 percent to 76.1 percent for all women between 1978 and 1987; they increased from 58.9 percent to 71.9 percent for poor women. In short, both the CPS-CSS and the OCSE show quite a strong improvement in child support enforcement for children dependent on welfare.

That we should find the most improvement in child support enforcement among the children on welfare is not surprising. To date, most of the dollars and legislative effort have been targeted at this group.

PROSPECTS FOR THE LONG RUN

Overall, the prospects for large long-run increases in child support payments are good. The difference between what is currently collected and what nonresident parents can afford to pay, according to the two most widely used standards in America, is enormous. Many of the policies that will increase payments are already on the books. Some of them, such as the utilization of numerical child support standards and routine income withholding, cost very little or might even save money.

On the other hand, some policies that would lead to large increases in child support payments would require nontrivial investments of funds. Getting from the current situation of paternity establishment as the exception to a situation in which paternity is established and a child support award is secured in the overwhelming majority of cases will be expensive, at least in the short run. And the change will come slowly. Similarly, unless child support awards are automatically updated by making them a percentage of the nonresident parent's income, it will be expensive to update them.

Furthermore, some policies that could lead to substantial increases in child support collections remain to be implemented, and others have yet to be enacted. Of those enacted but not yet fully implemented, we have seen that judicial discretion may undermine child support standards. For states to successfully implement routine withholding they must establish the bureaucratic machinery to receive and disburse child support payments. Only seven states had this capacity as of early 1992. Finally, neither the federal government nor any state had yet enacted an assured child support benefit.

Can child support collections be increased by a sufficient amount to finance a cost-neutral, assured, child support benefit of $2,000? Yes, but only with constancy. Collections can increase substantially if routine withholding and child support standards are implemented effectively and reinforced by future expenditures and legislation.

In the next chapter I will begin to discuss in detail the reasons behind the design choices of each element of the CSAS, beginning with the child support standard. In this way, I hope to illustrate the delicate balance among the standard, the withholding, and the assured benefit and how all three are necessary to improving child support payments.

NOTES

1. Oellerich, Garfinkel, and Robins, "Private Child Support," p. 20.
2. This figure is calculated by dividing the amount paid by the amount owed for each individual in the 1985 Current Population Survey-Child Support Supplement. It is lower than the figure obtained by dividing the total amount paid by all individuals by the total amount owed by all individuals, because, in general, those with high obligations pay a larger proportion of what they owe than those with low obligations.

3. Oellerich, Garfinkel, and Robins, "Private Child Support," Table 2, pp. 3–24. (The figure for the increase in awards is not presented in the table but is derived from figures given in the table by multiplying the maximum potential obligation of those without awards times the ratios of current awards to current collections and current obligations to obligations under the Wisconsin standard.)

4. Although some nonresident parents with no legal obligation to pay child support do, in fact, provide some, the proportion of those who provide anything without being obliged to by an award is much less than the proportion of those with child support awards, 18 percent versus 73 percent. Furthermore, the average amount paid by those without a legal obligation to pay is less than one-eighth of the amount paid by those with an obligation. These data are from computer runs by Carole Roan from the National Survey of Families and Households.

5. U.S. Bureau of the Census, "Child Support and Alimony: 1985" (Supplemental Report), Current Population Reports, Special Studies Series P-23, No. 154, March 1989, Table 2. Of those not awarded child support, about 6 percent give as the reason that a final award is pending. They are likely to get one and, so, are added to the cases with awards.

6. C. Wade and C. Tavris, *Psychology*, New York: Harper Collins, 1990.

7. U.S. Bureau of the Census, "Child Support and Alimony: 1985," Table 2.

8. Conversation with Michael Infranco, Deputy Commissioner, Office of Child Support Enforcement, New York City.

9. Edward M. Young, *Costs and Benefits of Paternity Establishment: Final Report*, The Center for Health and Social Services Research, Pasadena, California, Washington, D.C.: Center for Health and Social Services Research, 1985.

10. See Cassetty, *Child Support and Public Policy:* Gilbert Y. Steiner, *The Futility of Family Policy*, Washington, D.C.: The Brookings Institution, 1981, pp. 111–128.

11. Irwin Garfinkel and Annemette Sorensen, "Sweden's Child Support System: Lessons for the United States," *Social Work*, Vol. 27, No. 6 (November 1982), pp. 509–515.

12. Ann Nichols-Casebolt and Irwin Garfinkel, "Trends in Paternity Adjudications and Child Support Awards," *Social Science Quarterly*, Vol. 72, No. 1 (March 1991), Table 1, pp. 83–97.

13. Nichols-Casebolt and Garfinkel, *Trends.* A 50 percent increase in any rate during a six-year period is a respectable rate of change.

14. These statistics and those that follow on the proportions of mothers who want and do not want child support awards are taken

from U.S. Bureau of Census, *Child Support and Alimony: 1985,* Table C, p. 3.

15. U.S. Bureau of the Census, *Child Support and Alimony: 1985,* Table C, p. 3.

16. Oellerich, Garfinkel, and Robins, "Private Child Support," Table 2, pp. 3–24.

17. Jessica Pearson, Nancy Thoennes, and Patricia Tjaden, "Legislating Adequacy: The Impact of Child Support Guidelines," *Law and Society Review,* Vol. 23, No. 4, 1989, pp. 569–590.

18. This assumes that earnings of nonresident parents increase by 5 percent per year and that, in any given year, one-third of the orders are up to date, one-third are one year behind, and another third are two years behind.

19. Krause, *Child Support in America,* p. 25.

20. Harry D. Krause, "Child Support Reassessed: Limits of Private Responsibility and the Public Interest," *University of Illinois Law Review,* Vol. 9, No. 2, 1989, pp. 367–398; David L. Chambers, "The Coming Curtailment of Compulsory Child Support," *Michigan Law Review,* Vol. 80, 1982, pp. 1614–1634.

21. Ray L. Weaver and Robert G. Williams, "Problems with URESA: Interstate Child Support Enforcement Isn't Working but Could," paper presented at The American Bar Association Third Child Support Conference, Washington, D.C.: American Bar Association, 1989, p. 510.

22. U.S. Department of Health, Education and Welfare, Office of Child Support Enforcement, *Child Support Enforcement,* 13th Annual Report to Congress, Vol. 2, September 1988, pp. 16 and 34.

23. U.S. House of Representatives, *Background Material and Data on Programs,* pp. 662–667.

24. See Philip K. Robins, "Why Did Child Support Award Levels Decline from 1978 to 1985?" *Journal of Human Resources,* Vol. 27, No. 2 (Spring 1992) pp. 362–379. Oellerich, Garfinkel, and Robins, "Private Child Support," pp. 3–24; Andrea H. Beller and John W. Graham, "Child Support Payments: Evidence from Repeated Cross Sections," in *The American Economic Review: Papers and Proceedings of the One-Hundredth Annual Meeting,* American Economic Association, Vol. 78, No. 2, 1988, pp. 81–85.

25. See D. Oellerich, Garfinkel, and Robins, "Private Child Support," pp. 3–24.

26. Robins, "Why Did Child Support Award Levels Decline?"

27. U.S. Bureau of the Census, *Child Support and Alimony: 1981* (Advance Report), Current Population Reports, Special Studies Series P-23, No. 124, 1983, Table 1; U.S. Bureau of the Census, *Child Support and Alimony: 1987,* Current Population Reports, Special Studies Series P-23, No. 167, 1990, Table A.

28. The best measure of how well the child support enforcement system is doing compares total child support collections to what total collections would be if all potentially eligible children received the amounts prescribed by current standards. Donald Oellerich estimated that, according to the Colorado child support guidelines in 1978, Americans were collecting 23.9 percent of what should have been collected. By 1985 this percentage had slipped to 21.8 percent. According to the Wisconsin child support guidelines, collection effectiveness decreased over the same period from 21.4 percent to 18.8 percent. Given the large increase in collections in 1987, it is likely that collection effectiveness in 1987 was higher than in 1978, but Oellerich didn't include 1987 in his analysis. See Donald Oellerich, "Measuring National and State Performance Pursuing Private Child Support," June 1991, mimeo.

5 / Determining A Child Support Standard

There are two major philosophical approaches to determining child support standards: Cost sharing and income sharing.[1] Cost-sharing standards calculate the child support award on the basis of estimates of the cost of raising a child; income-sharing standards calculate awards on the basis of the incomes of the parents. States are now required to have a legislated formula for determining awards, and all of them use some sort of income-sharing standard. The two most common standards are the *income-shares standard* and the *percentage-of-income standard*. Although both are compatible with the CSAS, I prefer the percentage-of-income standard (even though most states are now using the income-shares standard). In this chapter, I will compare the designs of these two standards and explain the reasons for my preference.

APPROACHES TO NORMATIVE STANDARDS

Any normative standard for child support must attempt to balance the needs of the child, the nonresident parent, the resident parent, and society. There are two common approaches to translating the responsibility of child support into monetary terms: cost sharing and income sharing.

Cost Sharing

Cost sharing was used in the old system in which judges decided awards on a case-by-case basis. Calculations were based on the budget submitted by the resident parent. Courts reviewed that budget, sometimes adjusting it downward if they found that particular expenditures were not in keeping with the family's standard of living prior to divorce. Once the budget for the child was set, the court examined the nonresident parent's living costs and income to determine how much that parent was able to pay. The courts operated on the premise that the nonresident parent was entitled to a reasonable life-style based on his income, with the child receiving some of what was left over. The rationale for this gentle treatment of nonresident parents was the fear that oppressive settlements would result in evasion, and the child would then receive nothing.

When cost sharing is used as the basis for a normative standard, instead of in case-by-case decisions, setting an award amount is complicated by the fact that the cost of raising a child differs considerably depending on the income of the parent. Parents with higher incomes spend more money on their children, so setting an award amount unrelated to the income of the parents is virtually impossible. Thus, no states have adopted standards based on a pure cost-sharing approach.

With the income-sharing approach, because what is available to be shared depends upon the nonresident parent's income, that income is used as a starting point. If parents with more income spend more on their children, a standard should incorporate this sharing of income by the nonresident parent.

Income Sharing

The income-shares standard was first used by the state of Washington and then refined and developed by Robert G. Williams in a study commissioned by the federal Office of Child Support

Enforcement.[2] It is quite complex. The basic child support obligation is computed by multiplying the combined income of both parents by percentages that decline as income increases. The amount for one child, for example, ranges from 21.5 percent for incomes between $5,976 and $11,800 to 11.8 percent for incomes over $64,250. The total child support obligation is determined by adding actual work-related, child-care expenses and extraordinary medical expenses to the basic obligation. So, although it is based on income sharing, the income-shares approach has elements of cost sharing because it takes these expenses into account. The total obligation is then prorated between each parent, based on their individual incomes. The resident parent's obligation is assumed to be met in the course of everyday sharing with the child. The nonresident parent's obligation is payable as child support.

Under the income-shares approach, the nonresident parent's child support obligation declines as a percentage of his income when the total income of both parents increases. This means, in practice, that the amount the nonresident parent pays varies, depending on the resident parent's income. According to one classification, thirty-two states and Guam have adopted a form of the income-shares guideline, but some of these amount to an amalgam of the income-shares and percentage-of-income standard.[3]

As noted, the percentage-of-income standard is the one I recommend for the CSAS. Under it, the child support obligation is equal to a fixed percentage of the nonresident parent's income, varied by the number of children owed support. The standard has its roots in a system developed by the Michigan Friend of the Court, a public bureaucracy that enforces private child support orders. It is now most closely associated with Wisconsin because that is the state it was developed for, and Wisconsin was the first to use it. Composed of a fixed percentage of the nonresident parent's income, varied by the number of children to be supported, the child support award automatically adjusts for the fact that children in high-income families receive more than children whose parents have less to spend. Nine states, including Wisconsin, use this form of standard. Eight other states use a modified version of it: a percentage of the nonresident parent's income, varied according to the level of income.[4]

DETERMINING THE PERCENTAGES

How does one determine how much income a nonresident parent should share with his child? There are two possible solutions to this problem. One that has intuitive appeal is to set the nonresident parent's share at a rate that would equalize the incomes of the two households. This type of income sharing is known as income equalization and was proposed by Judith Cassetty and Isabel Sawhill.[5] The objective of such an approach is to ensure that the children continue to have the same standard of living as the nonresident parent. Because it is impossible to separate the standard of living of the child from that of the resident parent, income equalization also equalizes the standard of living of the parents. This entails substantially greater child support obligations for most upper-middle- and upper-income nonresident parents than do other standards. Although income equalization has been advocated by some academics, it has not been adopted by a single state.

The second approach to determining how much a parent ought to pay in child support is to base the amount on the proportion of their income that parents shared with their children when they all lived together. This is the starting point that I used with Marygold Melli when writing the percentage-of-income standard and that Robert Williams used when writing the income-shares standard. The manner in which the authors of the two standards arrived at the child's share differed, however, in two respects: (1) in the estimation of the percentage of income that two-parent families devote to their children, and (2) in the value judgments made when translating how parents share income in intact families to how they should share income when they live apart.

Determining how much of their income parents should share with children is far more complex and difficult than it appears. Although a considerable body of economic literature on the problem exists, research has not been able to tell us the exact proportion of their income that parents share with their children, because so many expenses, such as food, housing, and transportation, are jointly consumed. Determining how these common expenditures are allocated among individual members of the family is the principal stumbling block.

The architects of the income-shares approach calculated their percentages for the child support standard using one study of expenditures on children, that of Thomas J. Espenshade.[6] The authors merely extrapolated from the estimated percentages of expenditures on children given in Espenshade's study of two-parent families, to arrive at percentages for their standard.

In determining the Wisconsin percentage-of-income standard, we wrestled with the problem of what constitutes a child's equitable share. As part of the child support research conducted by the Institute for Research on Poverty under a contract from the Wisconsin DHSS, Jacques Van der Gaag conducted a comprehensive review of the economics literature on expenditures on children.[7] A dozen studies were reviewed, and we used Van der Gaag's findings as a starting point for recommending the percentages to be used in the standard. One of his major findings was that the range of estimates of the share of income that parents devote to their children is enormous. Even after limiting the studies to those he judged to be the most theoretically and methodologically sound, Van der Gaag found that the estimates of the proportion of income devoted to the first child ranged from 16 percent to 24 percent. Van der Gaag concluded that taking the midpoint of this range, 20 percent, was the best point estimate. But he cautioned "other observers might easily reach a different point estimate."[8] The most recent review of the literature on the costs of children, commissioned by the federal government, supports Van der Gaag's conclusion that the range of the scientifically valid studies is wide.[9]

Van der Gaag also found that expenditures on children were proportional up to very high income levels and that the shares of income devoted to the second and third child were about half that devoted to the first.

The economics data provided only the starting point for determining the percentages to be used in the Wisconsin standard. We recognized that, even if it were possible to calculate what proportion of income is shared in a two-parent household, that doesn't necessarily mean that a child in a broken home should receive exactly the same proportion of parental income. For example, some argue that nonresident parents should share a lower proportion of their incomes than they would share if they were living with the children. One reason this is argued is because a parent derives less benefit from a child when he or she lives apart from that child. Also, the nonresident parent incurs some costs in the course of normal visitation. Finally, child support orders that are too high a percentage of the nonresident parent's income may preclude a decent standard of living for the nonresident parent and, therefore, encourage evasion.

The other side of this argument is that nonresident parents should share more than they would if they still lived with the child, because it costs more to set up two separate homes. In an intact family, the child, as well as the parent, derives the full benefits of living in a nice house, for example, at no extra cost to the parent. To keep the child at this same standard of living, the nonresident's share must be greater than if the family still lived in a single household.

None of these reasons for expecting nonresident parents to share more (or less) income with their children suggests an exact amount or percentage. Ultimately, the decision about how much the nonresident parent should pay depends upon value judgments about how to balance the objectives of child support. Establishing a child support standard cannot be a purely scientific exercise.

In designing a standard for the CSAS, the joint Institute for Research on Poverty–Department of Health and Social Services working group that I headed considered the reasons for expecting nonresident parents to share both more and less of their income with their children. In addition, we sought to balance the objectives of providing for the children, being fair to the resident parent, minimizing public costs, and retaining incentives and a decent standard of living for the nonresident parent. Our final recommendation to the state was that the sharing rate for nonresident parents with one child be equal to 17 percent of gross income, a bit lower than Van der Gaag's best point estimate of 20 percent. The committee felt that the reasons for having a lower sharing rate for nonresident parents than for resident parents outweighed those for having a higher sharing rate.

Van der Gaag's estimates indicated that the expenditures for two children were about one and one-half those for only one child.

This suggested to the committee that, if the rate for one child equaled 17 percent, the rate for two should equal 25 percent. In considering the rates for three and more children, the committee tried to strike a balance between keeping the aggregate rate from getting too high and increasing the sharing rate for additional children. The committee's resolution was to recommend rates of 29, 31, and 34 percent for three, four, and five or more children, respectively.

One final note: Studies done to date have failed to take account of the potential income that a family forgoes when one parent, usually the mother, works less and earns less in the market, in order to care for the children. As Van der Gaag showed, this implicit cost of raising a child may be larger than the explicit costs of raising a child that are included in the studies of expenditures on children.[10] Ignoring this cost of child raising brings up questions about even the modest claim that the share of income that children would have received if the parents lived together is a reasonable starting point for determining how much child support should be paid. For standards that make the claim that the child should get the exact share she or he would have enjoyed if the parents lived together, ignoring this cost makes the exercise a mockery

THE UNFAIRNESS OF REGRESSIVE PERCENTAGES

One of the critical differences between the percentage-of-income standard and the income shares standard is that, in the former, the percentage of the nonresident parent's income to be paid in child support remains fixed, whereas, in the latter, the percentage declines substantially as income increases.[11]

Both the proportionality of the percentage-of-income standard and the regressivity of the income-shares standard were originally justified by their architects as reproducing the pattern of income sharing extant when children live with both parents. Van der Gaag's review, which guided our choices for the percentage-of-income standard, concluded that the proportion of income devoted to children was relatively constant up to very high income levels. In contrast, the report to the federal Office of Child Support

Enforcement on which the income-shares standard is based, concluded that the proportion of income that parents spend on their children declines as income increases.

The evidence presented in the report to the federal OCSE is unconvincing. Of the five studies the report reviews, only Espenshade's supports its conclusion. Of the other four, three fail to examine how the costs of children vary with income and the other finds the costs to be roughly proportional. One out of five is hardly solid evidence for rejecting the proportionality assumption.

The recently commissioned federal study on child costs and child support guidelines concludes that both the regressivity of the income-shares standard and the proportionality of the percent-of-income standards are consistent with the broad range of scientifically reliable estimates of the costs of children.[12]

That the scientific evidence on expenditures on children is consistent with either standard makes acutely clear the inescapability of making value judgments in designing a child support standard. I suspect that, once the value judgments implicit in the two standards are made explicit, the flat percentage-of-income standard, up to some income cap, will have wider appeal than the declining percentages in the income-shares standard. Regressive taxes are unfair. A regressive child support standard is too. It is hard to justify legislation that requires a working-class, nonresident parent to contribute a much larger proportion of his income to his children than a middle-income, nonresident parent and that requires the middle-income, nonresident parent to contribute a much larger share of his income than the upper-middle-income nonresident parent.

THE COSTS AND BENEFITS OF SIMPLICITY

The best argument for the percentage-of-income standard is its simplicity. Being equal to a percentage of the nonresident parent's income, the award varies only with the number of children owed support. The income-shares standard is more complex: The percentages of support owed vary with the income of both nonresident and resident parent and also depend upon expenditures on child care and medical care.

Simplicity in this case not only makes it easier for everyone to understand what to expect, but also eases the burden of administration. Most people who have either read or heard about the Wisconsin percentage-of-income standard, for example, understand it. Parents who enter the court system in Wisconsin have no difficulty assessing how much their entitlements or obligations will be. In contrast, even though the income-shares standard is not the most complex standard that exists, and indeed entails only a few more variables than the Wisconsin standard, it is far more difficult to understand. Just test the relative complexity of the two standards by attempting to calculate what your own obligation or entitlement would be under each standard.

Because the percentage standard is so simple, courts can easily administer it, thereby speeding up the process. It would be equally easy for social security or revenue departments to administer, if and when child support is transferred to one of these agencies.

Does simpler mean more fair, though? That is a more complicated issue. To the extent that fairness and equity depend upon tailoring child support awards to the unique circumstances of each case, simplicity is obviously the enemy of equity. The United States, however, has adopted the position that equity is better served by the rough-average justice produced by numerical child support standards. Indeed, a look at the legislation of the 1980s reveals a trend toward simplifying procedures by applying uniform formulas to everything from child support standards to taxes. The Tax Reform Act of 1986 was also based upon the presumption that simplicity promotes equity.

Trusting to congressional trends isn't always the best way to get the right answer, however. A general presumption that simplicity promotes equity is no substitute for examination of the consequences of the specific differences in simplicity between the two standards. The percentage-of-income standard is simpler insofar as it ignores the resident parent's income and takes no account of expenditures for child care and medical care. Examining the costs and benefits of both design choices in comparing the two standards will help show why, ultimately, the percentage-of-income standard is best.

WHY CHILD SUPPORT SHOULD NOT DEPEND ON THE INCOME OF THE RESIDENT PARENT

The most controversial aspect of the percentage-of-income standard is the fact that it does not take into account the income of the resident parent. In this it represents a complete break with past practice. In traditional family law, the financial resources of the resident parent played a critical role in determining child support. That law was based on a cost-sharing approach based on assessment of the needs of the child and the ability of the supporter to pay. It was assumed that, the more income the resident parent had, the more of the child's needs were already being met with this income and, therefore, the less child support was necessary from the nonresident parent to fulfill the remaining unmet needs.

The income-sharing approach assumes that both parents have an obligation to share their income with their children. To emphasize this dual obligation, the percentage-of-income standard does not consider the income of the resident parent at all in setting the amount the nonresident parent should pay. Making the nonresident parent's obligation contingent on the income of the resident parent undermines the dual obligation.

Additionally, the child is entitled to a share of both parents' incomes. When the parents live together, the child shares the benefits (and bears some of the costs as well) if both parents work. There is no evidence that the share of income the child receives from his or her father declines if the mother goes to work. A child in a single-parent household with two income-producing parents should enjoy the advantages of two earners as much as does a child in an intact family.

Furthermore, the income of the resident parent depends in large part upon how much she works. At the same time, the more the resident parent works, the greater the child care costs. If the resident parent's income *is* to be counted in determining the obligation of the nonresident parent, child care expenses cannot be ignored. The income-shares standard does take account of child care expenditures, but, as we will see shortly, doing so muddies the income-sharing principle by inserting a dose of cost sharing.

This inclusion also substantially complicates the determination and updating of child support awards.

The income-shares standard is also based on the philosophy that both parents have an obligation to share with their children. But, because of the way the award is calculated, the child support obligation of the nonresident parent declines as the income of the resident parent increases, similarly to traditional family law. This is only an accidental by-product of the fact that the percentage to be paid as child support declines as the total income of both parents increases. What if further research indicates, as I suspect it will, that the amount of money parents spend on their children does remain proportional to their income and if the income-shares model were adjusted to reflect that finding? If the percentage in the income-shares standard were constant, rather than declining, the income of the resident parent would play no role in determining the obligation of the nonresident parent. Indeed, if the percentage of family income spent on children increased with the income, the income-shares standard would lead to the absurd result that, the higher the income of the resident parent, the greater the child support obligation of the nonresident parent. This is not generally perceived and, therefore, is worth explaining.

Recall that, under the income-shares standard, the child support obligation is computed by multiplying the combined income of both parents by percentages that are determined by how much of their income two-parent families spend on their children. The obligation is then prorated between the parents, based on their proportionate shares of income. The nonresident parent's obligation is the child support award. (To simplify the calculations, we ignore child care expenses and extraordinary medical expenses.)

Suppose that research showed that two-parent families at all income levels spent 20 percent of their income on one child. Consider a case in which the nonresident father has a $20,000 income and the resident mother has a $10,000 income. Their total income is $30,000. The total child support obligation is $6,000. His share is two-thirds of the total, or $4,000. Now suppose that the resident mother's income is $20,000. Total income would now be $40,000. The total obligation is $8,000. But the father's share is only one-half the total, or, once more, $4,000! In other words, according to the income-shares standard, resident-parent income would be irrelevant in determining the child support obligation of the non-resident parent if income spent on children were found to be proportional rather than regressive. What if research showed that families with incomes below $40,000 spent 20 percent on their children, and those with $40,000 or more spent 25 percent of their income on their children? In the example just given, as the income of the resident mother increasaed from $10,000 to $20,000, the child support obligation of the nonresident father would increase from $4,000 to $5,000—an absurd result.

There may, of course, be arguments for taking the resident parent's income into account when setting the amount of a child support award. Certainly failure to consider it can lead to what appear to be inequitable results, especially in extreme cases. The argument is that, although it is fair for a nonresident parent earning $20,000 to pay $3,400 (17 percent) in child support if the resident parent has no income, it is unfair to expect the nonresident parent to pay the same amount if the resident parent earns $60,000. Whether these circumstances overcome the income-sharing principle of child support, those setting public policy must decide. But taking resident parents' incomes into account in the unsatisfactory manner of the income-shares standard is not the answer.

WHY CHILD SUPPORT SHOULD NOT DEPEND ON EXTRAORDINARY EXPENDITURES

Under the income-shares standard, child support obligations depend upon actual child care expenditures and extraordinary expenditures for medical care. These kinds of actual expenditures are irrelevant in the percentage-of-income standard.

Numerous objections can be raised to basing child support obligations on actual expenditures. To begin with, the practice is inconsistent with the income-sharing principle underlying both the income-shares and the percentage-of-income standard. To base obligations on actual expenditures is to rely upon cost sharing and income sharing.

How much the resident parent spends on child care depends on both the kind and amount of care purchased, which is largely determined by how much the resident parent works. What is the justification for increasing the child support paid by the nonresident parent in response to the resident parent's increases in work? It is difficult to think of one. After all, the more the resident parent works, the more income she will have.

Adjusting the child support obligation in response to truly extraordinary expenditures for medical care seems more appropriate. Such expenditures are presumably involuntary, and, in the rare cases of medical catastrophe, the average cost of medical care incorporated in a child support standard would be totally inadequate. It is hard to make the case that the resident parent should bear the entire cost of a medical catastrophe. But the real issue here is that *no* family should bear the entire cost. America's failure to institute a national health insurance system creates pressures to twist the child support system out of shape to compensate for a broader social problem.

The primary reason not to base the child support obligation upon actual expenditures for child care and medical care is that it further complicates the determination of child support. Such expenditures change substantially from year to year. Should this year's child support be based upon last year's expenditures? Or upon anticipated expenditures during the year? It is important to consider that every complication makes it more costly and difficult to update child support awards.

SUMMARY OF THE COSTS AND BENEFITS OF SIMPLICITY

The preceding analysis revealed how the designs of the two standards effect the ultimate equitability of each. It is clear that neither is ideal. Although having one constant percentage is more equitable than having declining percentages, ignoring the income of the resident parent may entail some sacrifice in equity. Although ignoring child care costs entails no sacrifice in, and probably promotes, equity, ignoring catastrophic medical care costs does entail sacrifice. In terms of the specifics, therefore, the verdict on whether the greater simplicity of the percentage-of-income standard promotes equity appears mixed. To the extent that the simplicity of the percentage-of-income standard substantially facilitates the updating of child support awards, however, the relationship between simplicity and equity is substantially strengthened.

Recall that one of the widely perceived problems with the U.S. child support system is that child support awards are too low and that a large part of the problem of low awards is attributable to the failure to update them over time.

Why are modifications of child support awards so rare? For one, most state laws adopted practices and legislation to discourage parents from seeking modifications of child support orders. These divorce guidelines suggest a modification, "only upon a showing of changed circumstances so substantial and continuing as to make the terms unconscionable."[13] But to say that laws and regulations discourage modifications begs the question. What is the rationale for this discouragement? Under the old system of individualized determinations of child support awards, modifications were quite costly in terms of court time. Updating a child support award was equivalent to reopening and rehearing the case. So, if the average child support case had a ten-year-obligation life, annual modification or updating under the old system would have increased the burden on the courts tenfold.

Numerical child support standards reduce the administrative burden of both establishing the initial child support award and modifying or updating the award over time, because of the simplicity of the standards. The more complex the standard, the greater the information the court or administrative agency must obtain, verify, and process, all of which is costly, even in this age of computers.

To illustrate the difference in the costs of updating a child support award derived from Wisconsin's percentage-of-income standard, as opposed to one derived from the income-shares standard, consider what actions a child support agency would have to take under the two standards. Take the most common case, in which both the nonresident and the resident parent are employed wage earners who receive no unearned income. Under the Wisconsin standard, the child support agency notifies the nonresident parent's employer of the percentage of income to be withheld and forwarded to the agency.[14] As the income of the nonresident parent increases (or decreases) over time, the child support withheld and paid also changes automatically. The only additional action the child support agency must take is to verify the income tax returns of the nonresident parent each year to ascertain if he has secured any additional sources of earned or unearned income. (Even this is rarely done.)

Even though the income-shares standard has only a few more variables than the Wisconsin percentage-of income standard, updating of awards entails a substantially greater administrative burden. Each year the child support agency must collect information from the income tax returns of both the resident and the nonresident parent, as well as information from the resident parent on the costs of child care and medical care. Some method of securing and verifying data on these expenditures has to be developed. The records of the two parents must be linked. Each year a new child support obligation must be calculated. Because only the child support agency as all the data upon which the revised child support obligation can be based, it has to notify the employer, the resident parent, and the nonresident parent of the new obligation every year.

Updating of the income-shares standard is feasible but substantially more costly than updating of the percentage-of-income standard. Consequently, it would at the very least, delay implementation of updating. It is even conceivable that the extra administrative burdens imposed by the income-shares standard could permanently discourage updating. And, although there is current strong political support for strengthening child support enforcement, the political euphoria over this may not last forever. Updating is essential to the CSAS as a way of assuring that child support awards are adequate, and this makes the simplicity of the percentage-of-income standard especially attractive.

SUMMARY AND CONCLUSION

This chapter has compared the two most popular types of child support standards. I continue to feel that the simplicity of the percentage-of-income shares standard used in Wisconsin is what makes it best for the CSAS as a whole. More states, however, currently use the income-shares standard, which is still a substantial improvement over no standard.

Both standards begin with the philosophical premise of income sharing: that to parent a child is to incur a responsibility to share income with the child, specifically the proportion that would have been shared if the nonresident parent still lived with the child. The standards depart from one another in application, however, because estimates of the extent and nature of income sharing in two-parent families vary widely and because a host of other value judgments must be made to derive child support orders. Under the income-shares approach, the child support obligation declines as a percentage of the nonresident parent's income as total income increases, and, consequently, the obligation decreases as the resident parent's income increases. Moreover, the obligation also depends upon expenses for child care and medical care. In contrast, under the percentage-of-income standard, the obligation is a flat percentage of the nonresident parent's income and depends neither upon the resident parent's income nor upon expenses for child and medical care.

Economic research on two-parent families provides mixed evidence of whether the percentage of income spent on the children declines as incomes increase. Moreover, the proportion of income that would have been spent on the child if the parents had remained together is a useful starting point for determining the proportion of income a nonresident parent should share, but whether that should be the end point or not is a value judgment. My values are such that a proportional child support standard is more appealing than one that is regressive.

Similarly, whether the resident parent's income should affect the nonresident parent's child support obligation is principally a subjective choice. Counting a resident parent's income is consistent with the old cost-sharing approach of determining child support obligations and seems intuitively fair; yet ignoring the resident parent's income is consistent with the income-sharing philosophy underlying both standards. If both parents work in the two-parent family, the child shares the monetary gains along with the parents. Why should it be any different when the family is separated?

The income-shares model accepts this line of reasoning in principle, but because obligations as a percentage-of-income decline as the total income of both parents increases, in practice, obligations decline as the resident parent's income increases, which is more in keeping with the old cost-sharing approach. Further, the income-shares model attempts to take the resident parent's income into account, but it does so in an unsatisfactory manner. For instance, if the income-shares standard were adjusted so that the percentages were proportional instead of regressive, the resident parent's income would be irrelevant.

Adjusting the child support obligation to take account of the costs of child care and medical care departs from the income-sharing philosophy underlying both standards, brings back the old cost-sharing approach, and complicates the standard.

As I stated at the beginning of this section, the most attractive feature of the percentage-of-income standard is its simplicity. Simplicity promotes public comprehension, is at least consistent with equity, and facilitates updating of awards. The last function may be the most important single consideration for the states in the future when constructing mathematical child support standards. Failure to update awards is a major source of inadequate child support. A scheme to provide quick and efficient updating may become an essential tool for child support enforcement.

APPENDIX 5.A / CHILD SUPPORT OBLIGATIONS IN JOINT CUSTODY CASES

Should joint custody effect the child support obligation? Without a futher explanation of what is meant by joint custody, this question cannot be answered. Joint physical custody, in which the child lives a substantial period of time with both parents, is very rare. In Wisconsin, only 2 percent of the couples share physical custody. Joint legal custody, under which both parents share legal responsibility for making decisions about the child, is much more common and is growing. In Wisconsin, about 20 percent of the divorces involve joint legal custody.

Joint legal custody should have no effect whatsoever on the child support obligation because it has no implications for which parent cares and provides for the child. Joint physical custody does have important implications for the amount of the child support obligation. Imagine the following extreme case: The parents have identical incomes, the child spends half of the time with each parent, and each parent incurs equal out-of-pocket expenditures for the child. In this case, it is impossible to distinguish between the resident and nonresident parent. Each parent is both. Each parent's child support obligation should be equal, which is to say that the net obligation of each should be zero.

There is a huge range between this extreme example and normal visitation, which I define as the child's spending every other weekend and two weeks during the summer with the nonresident parent. Does sharing of care for the child have to be perfectly equal for there to be an adjustment in the child support obligation? What if the split is nearly equal, say 45 percent and 55 percent? Furthermore, should the child support obligation be reduced even in cases where the incomes of the parents are not equal? What if they are nearly equal? These kinds of questions led the architects of the Wisconsin percentage-of-income standard to modify it, as described next, in order to deal with joint and split custody cases.

Split custody refers to divorces in which each parent receives physical custody of at least one child. In principle, split and joint physical custody should be treated the same. Because it is simpler, we begin the discussion with split custody. In split custody cases, each parent is both a resident and a nonresident. Each incurs an obligation of 17 percent of her or his income for the child living with the other parent, 25 percent for two children living with the other parent. If the incomes and the number of children divided are equal, the obligations are equal and there is no net transfer. More often, however, the incomes or the number of children owed support differ, and there is a net transfer.

Joint physical custody is similar to split custody in that each parent is both a resident and nonresident. Each child's time is split. Calculation of the child support obligation in the joint physical custody case is complicated somewhat by the visitation issue. To simplify the calculation of child support obligations for the vast majority of cases, no reduction in the obligation of the nonresident parent should be made until his or her share of resident care exceeds normal visitation.

A more serious complication is that each parent's expenditures on the child may not be proportional to the time that each has physical custody. Food expenditures are likely to be proportional to time spent with each parent. But housing expenditures are more of a fixed cost. And, even if the child's time is divided equally between each parent, one parent may take responsibility for most clothing purchases. Despite this, I would recommend that courts, and in the future, administrative bodies, presume that expenditures are divided in proportion to the provision of residential care when they determine child support obligations in joint custody cases and inform the parents that this presumption underlies the calculation of the child support obligation and that any serious deviation from it would justify a modification of the award.

NOTES

1. The bulk of this chapter is taken from Irwin Garfinkel and Marygold Melli, "The Use of Normative Standards in Family Law Decisions: Developing Mathematical Standards for Child Support," *Family Law Quarterly*, Vol. 24, No. 2 (Summer 1990), pp. 157–178.
2. Advisory Panel on Child Support Guidelines and Robert G. Williams, *Development of Guidelines for Child Support Orders: Advisory Panel Recommendations and Final Report to U.S. Office of Child Support Enforcement*, Williamsburg, VA.: National Center for State Courts, September 1987.
3. The states are Alabama, Arizona, Colorado, Connecticut, Florida, Idaho, Indiana, Iowa, Kansas, Kentucky, Louisiana, Maine, Maryland, Michigan, Missouri, Montana, Nebraska, New Jersey, New Hampshire, New Mexico, New York, Ohio, Oklahoma, Oregon, Pennsylvania, Rhode Island, South Carolina, South Dakota, Utah, Vermont, Virginia, and Washington. This classification is not perfect and changes over time. New York, for example, is classified under the income-shares approach, which is correct except that no note is taken of the fact that the New York standard, like the Wisconsin standard, is a flat percentage of the nonresident parent's income. In this case, as shown in the text, the resident parent's income does not affect the child support obligation. In an earlier report, Munsterman found that, as of mid-1989, 24 states had adopted the income-shares approach, 13 had adopted the flat percentage-of-income approach, and another 11 had adopted a varying percentage-of-income standard (Janice T. Munsterman, *A Summary of Child Support Guidelines*, Arlington, Va.: National Center for State Courts Washington Project Office, February 1990).

4. Ibid. The nine states with the fixed percentage-of-income standard are Alaska, Georgia, Illinois, Mississippi, Nevada, North Carolina, Tennessee, Texas, and Wisconsin. The eight states with the varying percentage-of-income standard are Arkansas, California, District of Columbia, Massachusetts, Minnesota, North Dakota, Puerto Rico, and Wyoming.
5. See Judith Cassetty, *Child Support and Public Policy; Securing Support;* Sawhill, "Developing Normative Standards."
6. See Advisory Panel and Williams, *Development of Guidelines;* Thomas Espenshade, *Investing in Children: New Estimates of Parental Expenditures* (Washington, D.C.: Urban Institute Press, 1984). The 1987 report to the federal Office of Child Support Enforcement, which set forth the income-shares standard, justified ignoring the bulk of the existing economics literature on the grounds that the 1960s data upon which these studies are based was outdated. On this ground, the Espenshade study upon which the report relied exclusively can now be dismissed as well, because it was based on 1972 data and studies now available are based on data from the 1980s. But this line of reasoning has little scientific merit. There are no grounds for believing that the pattern of sharing between parents and their children has shifted radically since the 1960s.
7. Van der Gaag, "On Measuring the Costs," pp. 1–44.
8. Ibid., p. 21.
9. Laurie Bassi, Laudan Aron, Burt S. Barnow, and Abhay Pande, "Estimates of Expenditures on Children and Child Support Guidelines," report submitted to the Office of the Assistant Secretary for Planning and Evaluation, U.S. Department of Health and Human Services by Lewin/ICF, October, 1990.
10. Van der Gaag, "On Measuring the Costs," p. 31.
11. The architects of the Wisconsin standard recommended that the flat percentages apply only to the first $50,000 or $60,000 of income in 1980 dollars. In part, the recommendation was based on the Van der Gaag finding of proportionality only up to very high incomes. Another consideration was that the public interest in assuring children a share of their parents' income declined at very high income levels. The Wisconsin DHSS rejected the idea of an income cap to the standard, but the legislature was more flexible. As adopted, the statute 767.25 (1M) (1987–88) allows the court to depart from the standard when it finds that use of the percentage standard is unfair to any of the parties. Presumably this would cover cases in which the nonresident parent's income is unusually high.
12. Bassi, Aron, Barnow, and Pande, "Estimates of Expenditures."
13. Uniform Marriage and Divorce Act 316, 9A U.L.A. (1979).

14. This example assumes that the initial child support order is expressed in percentage terms rather than in dollar terms, which is as yet true in only a minority of cases in the state. Most of the courts have been reluctant to issue percentage orders because no mechanism is in place to verify the income of the nonresident parent and, thereby, ascertain that the amount being withheld and forwarded by employers is correct.

6 / Designing an Assured Benefit

AN ASSURED BENEFIT: U.S. ATTEMPTS AND EUROPEAN PROGRAMS

In the United States, as of 1991, only Wisconsin and New York were entitled to receive federal funds to test an assured benefit in a pilot program. In Wisconsin, the pilot program has been held up by political infighting among changing administrations; in New York, a variant of an assured benefit, known as the Child Assistance Program (CAP), has been implemented in a very limited fashion in seven counties.[1]

Several European countries have what they call *advance maintenance benefits*, which are equivalent to an assured child support benefit. The Swedish advance maintenance system is one of the oldest and most developed.[2] In 1937 a law was passed in Sweden allowing a woman living with children whose father was absent and not paying child support to apply for advance maintenance payments. Such families received from the government the amount the father was obligated to pay. The government, in turn, became responsible for collecting the debt from the liable father. Amounts not collected were paid out of general revenue. Initially, eligibility for this program was limited to women who were too poor to provide for the children themselves. In addition, there had to be a legally liable father, which meant that paternity had to be established before advance maintenance was available.

In 1947 eligibility for the program was made independent of the custodial parent's income, and children with an unknown father became eligible after the age of three. The program was changed again in 1957 to include a guaranteed minimum payment for each child. Children whose noncustodial parents failed to pay support received this guaranteed minimum payment. Also, children who were supposed to receive less than this minimum according to the support agreement between their parents received the difference from the government, provided that the low private payment was due to the nonresident parent's inability to pay more. The government's guaranteed maintenance level was set at 40 percent of the official basic need of a child. Today, all children with an absent parent are entitled to advance maintenance, and noncustodial parents of children in the program are supposed to pay a standardized amount of support.

Denmark and Norway have had similar advance maintenance programs for decades. Recently, Germany, Austria, France, and some Swiss cantons developed more limited programs. The German program is typical of this group.[3] Children who are both eligible for child support and less than six years of age are entitled to receive an assured benefit for a maximum of three years, but eligibility is voided if the resident parent remarries.

The various European advance maintenance benefits, and even the differences in the proposed Wisconsin pilot program and the New York demonstration, reveal a wide variety of ways to implement an assured child support benefit. Eligibility, for instance, may depend only upon potential entitlement to child support (as it does in Sweden) or upon legal entitlement to child support (as it does in Wisconsin). Eligibility may also depend upon income (as it did in the early Swedish system) and even upon being an AFDC recipient (as it does in New York). Similarly, benefit levels may be high or low (recall the Swedish system again, in which the benefit is 40 percent of the estimated costs of a child's basic needs). The benefit may last throughout the child's minority or for only a few years (as it does in Germany). This chapter addresses a number of these kinds of issues of program design and demonstrates the balance of incentives that a well-crafted assured benefit can offer.

THE ASSURED BENEFIT PROPOSED FOR THE CSAS

Eligibility for an assured benefit would be limited to children legally entitled to receive private child support. Those eligible would receive either the award money that the nonresident parent pays or an assured child support benefit, whichever was higher. When nonresident parents paid less than the assured child support benefit level, the difference would be made up by the government. This benefit would be universal, not income tested. It would last until the child was nineteen.

Mothers on AFDC entitled to child support would still receive the first $50 of the award, and the rest of the award payment would still be used to offset AFDC costs. The assured benefit for mothers who have awards but aren't being paid would go entirely toward offsetting AFDC costs. When a mother stopped receiving AFDC benefits, she could then receive the assured benefit or the full child support payment, whichever was higher.

Initially I would set the benefit for one child at $2,000 to $2,500. Assured benefits for the second, third, fourth, fifth, and sixth child would equal $1,000, $1,000, $500, $500, and $500, respectively. Rather than an income-tested benefit, the public-subsidy portion of the assured benefit would be taxable income for the resident parent.

This plan was amended somewhat for the Wisconsin demonstration. Eligibility was still legal entitlement to private child support. But the assured benefit was set at $3,000 per year for one child and approximately $600 for each additional child. Benefits ceased to increase after the sixth child.

To reduce the costs of the program and to avoid paying any public benefits to high-income families, Wisconsin proposed a surtax on the income of the resident parent, which is referred to as the *resident parent contribution.* (See discussion later in the chapter of how the surtax crept into, and eventually perverted, the planned assured benefit demonstration in Wisconsin.) This contribution was calculated using the same rates imposed on the nonresident parent—17 percent of gross income for one child, and 25 percent, 29 percent, 31 percent, and 34 percent, respectively, for two, three, four, and five or more children—up to the amount of the public subsidy, after which it fell to zero. The effect of this surtax was to further restrict eligibility to families with incomes below $14,000 to $17,000, depending upon the number of children eligibile for support.[4]

In addition to the assured benefit, families eligible for child support with incomes of $8,000 or less would also have been eligible for a work expense subsidy equal to $1.00 per hour worked (up to a maximum of 2,000 hours) if there had been one child and $1.75 per hour worked if there had been two or more children. Between $8,000 and $16,000, the work expense subsidy was to have been reduced as income increased, so that at $16,000 the benefit would have been equal to zero.

ISSUES IN THE DESIGN OF AN ASSURED BENEFIT

Should the assured benefit be limited to those with legal entitlement to awards? Should it be income tested? How should we decide on the level of the benefit? The following sections examine these and other design questions.

Limiting Eligibility to Those with Awards

Limiting eligibility for the assured child support benefit to children legally entitled to receive private child support is essential to creating and preserving the system's integrity. Recall the philosophical underpinning: Parents are responsible for supporting their children and government is responsible for assuring that the children receive what they are entitled to. The assured benefit provides insurance for single mothers and a minor degree of redistribution. To dispense with legal entitlement to child support as an eligibility condition is to slight both parental responsibility and government responsibility to enforce awards in order to achieve a short-run increase in redistribution.

One of the key objectives of the child support assurance system is to provide a nonstigmatizing alternative to our current welfare system. We have seen that a large proportion of single mothers cannot earn their way out of poverty on their own even if they work full time. To attain a decent standard of living for their families, these mothers need to have their income supplemented. The CSAS is perfectly suited to providing income supplementation in a nonstigmatizing manner, *precisely because it is a child support system with only a minor degree of redistribution.* If the system slights the role of parental responsibility and highlights the redistributive element, it becomes more stigmatizing. The more clearcut the distinction between AFDC and the CSAS, the less scorn there will be for the CSAS. Eligibility for an assured benefit hinged on legal entitlement to private support is essential to creating a sharp distinction between the programs.

In addition to insuring the system's integrity and sharpening the distinction between the two programs, making eligibility for the assured benefit contingent upon legal entitlement to child support creates powerful incentives for establishing paternity and securing child support awards. Currently, over 70 percent of children born out of wedlock do not have child support awards. Creating incentives for this group to obtain them should help change this bleak picture.

Ineligible children. The critical argument against making legal entitlement to private child support the eligibility condition for the assured benefit is that doing so deprives the children without awards of this benefit. The children, after all, are blameless; their mothers may also be blameless. What if mothers are willing to cooperate with public officials to secure proof of paternity and a child support award, but officials simply don't have the time or resources to secure the award? Why punish these mothers and their children by denying them the opportunity to participate in the CSAS?

Current AFDC policy reflects this view. The AFDC program does not require that mothers be legally entitled to a child support award; it simply requires that mothers cooperate with public officials to establish paternity and locate fathers.

But this is an ineffective policy. Despite the cooperation requirement, paternity is not established in most AFDC cases. There are very few sanctions for mothers who fail to cooperate and very few "good-cause" exceptions. The cooperation requirement simply doesn't work in the majority of cases. The record for establishing paternity is so abysmally low that to lose the incentive for women to cooperate in this process just isn't worth it, even though it would do more to reduce poverty in the short run. It is more valuable to the CSAS as a whole to increase paternity identification in the long term than to make the assured benefit universally available to all single mothers right away.

Besides, as neither the assured benefit nor the CSAS would eliminate AFDC, imposing strict eligibility conditions on the assured benefit would not worsen the situation of any potential beneficiaries because they still have AFDC. If there were no welfare program upon which those not eligible for the CSAS could depend, the case against requiring legal entitlement as the condition of eligibility would be stronger. (Of course in exceptional cases when a pregnancy is the result of rape or incest and pursuing paternity would probably result in physical or emotional harm to the child or the mother, legal entitlement to child support could be waived. Under current AFDC regulations these are good-cause exceptions to the requirement that the mother cooperate in establishing paternity.)

In the future, when the overwhelming majority, say 95 percent, of those potentially eligible for child support actually have awards, the nation may want to loosen the requirements. At this point, however, so far from achieving universal paternity and award establishment, it is prudent to base eligibility on an objective outcome rather than on a subjective judgment by officials of the quality of the mother's contribution to the process.

Advantages of a Universal Assured Benefit

Currently, all of America's public transfer programs that provide benefits to children potentially eligible for child support—AFDC, Food Stamps, Medicaid, and Public Housing—are for the poor alone. To reduce the economic insecurity of families with children potentially eligible for child support, the nation should rely more heavily on universal programs, like free public education, Social

Security, Medicare, and the newly emerging child support collection system, that provide benefits to these families, whatever their incomes.

A non-income-tested, assured, child support benefit would prevent poverty and reduce the economic insecurity of the millions of children who, although not quite poor, suffer from large drops in income when their parents separate.

The income-tested benefit and work. If the assured benefit were income tested, it would discourage work among poor single mothers. To confine the assured benefit to those with low incomes, it must be reduced as the income of the resident parent increases. But reducing benefits as earnings increase is equivalent to taxing earnings and reduces the reward for work. In contrast, a universal benefit is not reduced as earnings increase. Thus, universal benefits give the greatest incentive for low-income mothers to work.

One of the serious problems with relying so heavily upon welfare programs is that they impose implicit tax rates (benefit reduction rates) on the poor that are higher than the tax rates required to finance the programs. This is equivalent to imposing regressive tax rates in the overall tax transfer system. Whereas the rich lose part of what they earn through taxes, the poor lose an even bigger part of what they earn through reductions in benefits. We fail to recognize this regressivity because it is imposed, not by institutions that tax all of us, but by special institutions that are designed to, and do, help the poor.

Because welfare programs lead to this regressivity, they are not a desirable means of supplementing the incomes of the poor who are expected to work. The poor can earn less in the market than the nonpoor. Regressive tax rates exacerbate this inequality; they stack the deck against the poor who try to achieve through hard work, the way Americans are "supposed" to achieve.[5] Hence, these rates reduce, rather than enhance, equality of opportunity. Furthermore, owing to their higher tax rates, welfare programs create greater incentives for the poor to work at intermittent, informal, and even illegal jobs from which the earnings need not be reported.

The segregation of the poor by income testing. Limiting the assured benefit to low-income families would also segregate them from other recipients. In universal programs, one bureaucracy deals with rich and poor alike, thereby integrating low-income beneficiaries into the social mainstream. Welfare, in contrast, creates special bureaucracies to deal with the poor alone.

The United States is now creating a public bureaucracy for enforcing private child support obligations for children from all income classes. Child support agencies will be mailing checks each month to the resident parent of children eligible for support. If the assured child support benefit is not limited to low-income families, it can be administered cheaply and efficiently by making the monthly checks no less than the assured child support benefit level. If, however, the assured benefit is limited to low-income families, there will need to be another new bureaucracy to check on incomes. Thus, another argument for not limiting the assured child support benefit to the poor is that, in terms of administration, it is more efficient.[6] Furthermore, confining the benefit to the poor stigmatizes it.

The appeal of income testing. There are two reasons people argue in favor of limiting eligibility for an assured benefit to low-income families. The first is cost: The lower the income eligibility level for the benefit, the fewer families will be eligible and the smaller the cost will be. The second reason is to avoid the horror cases of very wealthy families receiving a public subsidy.

The horror-case argument must be disposed of first, so that the cost issue can be considered more dispassionately. First, it is important to remember that nonresident parents associated with upper-income resident parents are usually themselves middle- or upper-income earners, and in these cases no public subsidy is involved. But there are exceptions. For example, what about the situation when a father who has substantial income gets custody of the children and the mother has little income? Or when a nonresident father is a low earner and the resident mother is a high earner or has remarried a high earner?

Recall that the primary goal of the CSAS is to prevent economic insecurity for all children. Very few Americans consider it shocking that Rockefellers collect social security benefits and are allowed to attend public schools for nothing. Is it a horror story when unemployed engineers from Boeing collect unemployment insurance? Quite the opposite! The unemployed Boeing engineer is suffering from economic insecurity. Unemployment insurance, like child support assurance, is designed to prevent impoverishment by relieving the distress of economic insecurity well short of poverty. Indeed, the so-called horror stories strengthen the integrity of non-income-tested benefits by clearly differentiating them from welfare. If Boeing engineers and even Rockefellers are entitled to the benefit it can hardly be welfare.

So long as the horror cases are rare exceptions rather than indicators of a more general perverse redistribution, they should not persuade Americans to limit benefits to those with low incomes. An assured child support benefit is clearly redistributive and will become even more so once child support awards are obtained more universally.

Costs are potentially a more serious matter. For example, I estimate that the extra cost of an income-tested assured benefit of $2,000 and $3,000 would be only $.2 billion and $.8 billion.[7] Compare these figures with the extra costs of a non-income-tested assured benefit of $2,000 and $3,000, which equals, respectively, $1.2 billion and $3.2 billion. In other words, income testing an assured benefit of $2,000 would save $1 billion; income testing an assured benefit of $3,000 would save $2.4 billion.

Although this is a substantial portion of the total estimated cost of the assured benefit, the total costs in either case are small. More important, the savings that arise from income testing are not worth the cost of what would be given up. An income-tested assured benefit would not provide security for the many people who are marginally poor, it would decrease incentives for welfare mothers to work (thereby increasing welfare dependence), and it would stigmatize the CSAS.

Eligibility Limited to AFDC Recipients

In the New York State demonstration of an assured benefit, the Child Assistance Program (CAP), initial eligibility depends not only upon having a child support award and being a resident of a county that is testing CAP, but also upon being eligible for AFDC.[8]

The CAP benefit was originally equal to $3,000 for one child and $1,000 for each additional child.[9] When AFDC benefits were increased in New York in 1990, CAP benefits were increased by a similar percentage, so that they were $3,360 for the first child and $1,120 for each additional child.

Once a family becomes eligible for CAP, the AFDC eligibility rules no longer apply. The CAP benefit is reduced by only ten cents for each dollar of the resident parent's income up to the poverty level and by sixty-six cents for each dollar of income in excess of the poverty level. This benefit reduction rate limits eligibility for CAP benefits to families with incomes below 1.5 times the poverty level. What this means in practice is that there are two different income eligibility levels for the assured benefit. To qualify for it initially, income must be low enough to qualify for AFDC. Once the family qualifies, however, income can rise above the AFDC eligibility level, and, so long as it doesn't exceed the assured benefit eligibility level of 1.5 times the poverty level, the family continues to receive an assured benefit.

The virtues of restricting eligibility to AFDC recipients are obvious. It reduces costs and targets the most needy for benefits, and it does so more effectively than by simply limiting the benefit to low-income families. But, again, are the savings worth the costs?

The previous section denoted how confining eligibility for the assured benefit to low-income families would vitiate the reductions in economic insecurity and welfare dependence that an assured child support benefit is capable of accomplishing. Making eligibility for the assured benefit contingent upon eligibility for AFDC benefits further erodes the ability of the assured benefit to reduce insecurity and dependence. It means that no help is provided to the millions of single mothers and their children who suffer from economic insecurity yet manage to avoid welfare dependence. Compared to Wisconsin's assured benefit, which has similar income limits but no requirement of AFDC eligibility, the New York plan achieves even less reduction in economic insecurity. Families must fall all the way down to the welfare level before they are offered any help.

Confining the assured child support benefit to AFDC recipients converts it from a nonwelfare alternative to an adjunct of the welfare system. As a consequence, it would achieve a much smaller reduction in welfare dependence. There are two reasons why an assured benefit would induce resident parents to leave welfare. The first is strictly economic. Because the assured benefit is not reduced as earnings increase, the economic incentives are better. The second is social. Because welfare recipients tend to be looked down upon and disdained, a nonwelfare benefit would induce them to leave welfare precisely to escape this contempt. Limiting the assured benefit to AFDC recipients tarnishes it. Thus, it would be much less attractive than a true alternative to welfare.[10] Perhaps most important, limiting eligibility to AFDC recipients precludes reductions in welfare dependence that would come from diverting families entirely from the welfare system. An assured child support benefit that is not dependent upon prior eligibility for AFDC would divert some families from ever becoming dependent on AFDC. Indeed, limiting eligibility to AFDC recipients creates an incentive for families to become eligible for AFDC and could, thereby, contribute to at least temporary increases in welfare dependence.

Cautionary Tales from Wisconsin about Income Testing

The corrosive impact of trying to target benefits better to low-income families is also illustrated by the Wisconsin experience. Proposed in a general form in 1978, the Child Support Assurance System, including the assured benefit, was to be available to all income classes.[11] In 1980, the Wisconsin DHSS contracted with the IRP to design a more detailed child support system for the state and to estimate its costs and benefits. In our 1982 report, Child Support: Weaknesses of the Old and Features of a Proposed New System, we recommended that the assured benefit be subject to a special surtax. The surtax envisioned was a small one that would have been administered through the income tax, but I had not clearly thought out the dimensions of the surtax. Despite my conviction that the assured benefit must remain universal, I was striving to make the system as a whole cost-neutral. This, plus the added complexity of simulating a benefit that was taxable according to conventional income tax rates, drove me in the direction of simulating a flat proportional tax. (Unfortunately, it was not until much later, after the political decision to adopt a surtax had already been made, that I simulated alternative tax rates.)

The flat proportional surtax was exactly the kind of surtax recommended to the Wisconsin DHSS by the Statewide Advisory Committee that the department had appointed (and on which I served) for advice on child support reforms. The committee recommended surtax rates equal to one-half the rates applied to the nonresident parent, or 8.5 percent for one child, 12.5 percent, 14.5 percent, 15.5 percent, and 17 percent for two, three, four, and five or more children, respectively. These rates implied that resident-parent families with two children eligible for child support would only receive a public subsidy so long as their incomes were below $28,000. (To obtain this figure, one simply divides the assured benefit for two children, $3,500, by the surtax for two children, 12.5 percent.)

To further reduce costs and the number of families that would receive the assured benefit, and to achieve the appearance of requiring equal contributions from resident and nonresident parents, in 1984 the Secretary of the Wisconsin DHSS, Linda Reivitz, elected to raise the surtax rates on the resident parent to the same level as the rates applied to the nonresident parent.

The surtax on the resident parent was renamed the *custodial parent contribution*. The public rationale for it was not so much that it reduced costs and caseloads, although these were the major concerns in the policy deliberations, but more that it promoted equity between custodial and nonresident parents by treating them equally. Both were expected to contribute equal percentages of their incomes to the child. The public subsidy was to come into play only in the event that the contributions from both parents were insufficient to cover the level of the assured benefit.

In the meantime, doubling the surtax rate, or the custodial-parent contribution, resulted in cutting the income eligibility level for the assured benefit in half or, for a family with two eligible children, to $14,000. Suddenly a moderate amount of income testing had been converted into a huge amount of income testing. The assured benefit had become a lot more like welfare.

Furthermore, the large custodial-parent contribution drove planners in the direction of administering it just like welfare. If the surtax on the incomes of resident parents were sufficiently small, it could be collected at the end of the year as a surtax on the income tax, but a large surtax makes this impossible because it imposes large obligations on families with low incomes. For example, a family with one child eligible for support and with only $10,000 in income would owe $1,700 in surtax at the end of the year. To expect such a low-income family to have $1,700 on hand at the end of the year is completely unrealistic (even $850 is probably too high). Consequently, planners recommended that, like welfare beneficiaries, resident parents be required to report their income to program administrators who would then calculate the custodial-parent contribution and net it out of the assured benefit payment.

Despite our intention to design a nonwelfare alternative to AFDC, therefore, a series of small compromises led to the assured benefit's becoming more like another welfare benefit. In 1988 I attempted to remedy this by proposing that the surtax be eliminated and the benefit be taxed as income, but my plea was denied, ironically, because it was thought any changes at the time would delay implementation.

The Assured Benefit and Remarriage

As mentioned earlier, Germany, like several European countries, discontinues advance maintenance payments when resident parents remarry. Because remarriage often reduces economic need, some U.S. policymakers suggest discontinuing the assured benefit when single parents marry. Limiting benefits to children with single parents is an alternative to limiting benefits to low-income families as a way to keep costs down. But it is not a very effective alternative. The microsimulation, laid out in chapter 3, of how much an assured benefit would cost in varying situations shows that, if eligibility for the assured benefit were limited to single parents, the poverty gap for families eligible for child support would decline by only 16 percent, rather than by 17 percent. Further, confining the benefits to single parents and excluding remarried parents would save only $.3 billion.[12]

There are several other arguments against discontinuing the assured benefit after remarriage. First, although the number of remarried couples whose families are poor is small, a much larger number are near poor. Second, to discriminate against these families is inequitable. Third, limiting the assured benefit to single-parent families would discourage remarriage. Discouraging remarriage would, in turn, further vitiate the reductions in economic insecurity and welfare dependence that an assured benefit can achieve. Marriage is the most important escape route from economic insecurity and welfare dependence for single mothers. Just as an assured benefit would make work more attractive to AFDC mothers, so too would it make remarriage more attractive. Moreover, an assured child support benefit would also make an AFDC mother a more economically attractive marriage partner. Thus, an assured benefit would increase the attractiveness of marriage to both parties and, thereby, lead to reductions in welfare dependence via remarriage. Confining benefits to single mothers would eliminate this effect.

Finally, private child support obligations do not terminate upon remarriage of the resident parent. Withdrawing the assured benefit feature of the child support assurance system upon remarriage makes no more sense. The analogy with survivors insurance is applicable here. Although benefits for the mother are discontinued upon remarriage, those for the children continue. The rationale for this was twofold. First, the stepparent has no legal obligation to support the children. Second, by continuing benefits for the children, remarriage is facilitated. Both arguments also apply to the CSAS.

Again, analysis of the costs and benefits of limiting the benefit reveals high costs and small gains. To target benefits and reduce costs, the best method is to tax benefits.[13]

Taxation of the Assured Benefit

Until recently, most government transfers were not taxable. Now, both old-age and unemployment insurance benefits are taxable. The rationale for exempting such income from taxation was that the beneficiaries were generally too poor to afford to pay income taxes. But this argument proved weak, because, if the income of beneficiaries is low enough, they have no income tax liability. If their other income is high enough to be taxable, families receiving government transfers can afford to pay taxes. Each dollar of transfers they receive increases their income by a dollar and, thereby, increases their ability to pay taxes by the same amount as a dollar from any other source. For this reason it is hard to justify a special exemption for any kind of transfer income. As a general principle, all income should be taxable. The argument for making the assured benefit taxable follows from these general considerations about good income tax policy.

Taxing the assured benefit is the best way to reduce the costs of the program and more precisely target benefits. Depending upon the existence and nature of state income taxes, making the benefit taxable reduces its value by between 30 percent and 40 percent for the few very wealthy people who qualify for it; reduces it by between 20 percent and 30 percent for the more numerous, comfortable, middle-class families who qualify for it; and reduces it by 10 percent to 20 percent for the even more numerous, lower-middle-class families who qualify. In short, it is an equitable way of applying an income test.

So, what is the difference if the income testing takes place within the assured benefit system or as part of the income tax system? All the difference in the world in terms of work incentives for the poor, social integration, and stigma. In the former case, low-income resident parents face much higher marginal tax rates. In the latter, a much larger group of lower-middle- and middle-income families face the same tax rate, but they pay slightly higher taxes because their taxable income increases by the amount of the public subsidy. In the former, there is a separate test of means within the benefit system to confine the benefits to low-income families. In the latter, the test of means takes place within the income tax in the context of a societywide test of means to determine ability to pay tax. Making Unemployment Insurance and old age and survivors insurance benefits taxable has not diminished the degree to which these benefits are perceived to be distinct from welfare.

Of course, simply making benefits taxable does not reduce costs as much as imposing income eligibility limits on benefit receipt.[14] My estimates suggest that the difference in cost for a $2,000 assured benefit in the intermediate run could amount to $1 billion.[15] But these additional savings can be achieved only at the cost of compromising the integrity of an assured child support benefit and converting it into just one more welfare benefit.

Choosing a Benefit Level

The Swedes keep the level of their advance maintenance payment at 40 percent of the estimated cost of a child's basic needs. Determining the appropriate level of the assured child support benefit is not an easy matter when designing for a U.S. system that lacks the social supports of the Scandinavians. Unlike with welfare, the assured benefit level should not be determined by the costs of raising a child. For, unlike with welfare, the assured child support benefit is not designed to assist families with no other income. Rather, the assured benefit is designed to supplement the earnings and other income of resident parents. As such, it need not be high enough to cover the cost of raising a child.

To determine the assured benefit level, we must consider the way the CSAS is designed to work as a whole. The higher the benefit level, the more the assured benefit would reduce poverty, economic insecurity, and welfare dependence. However, the higher the assured benefit, the greater the number of nonresident parents whose child support payments would be less than the assured benefit, and the more it would cost. In addition, the higher the assured benefit, the larger the redistributive element and the greater the danger that it would be perceived as a welfare benefit.

To avoid any possibility of the assured benefit's being perceived as a welfare benefit, Dr. Robert Lerman, an economist at American University who has advocated a child support assurance system, argued that the benefit level be set low enough, about $1,100 for one child, that the overwhelming majority (say 90 percent) of nonresident parents would be able to afford to pay it. If the assured benefit were no higher than nearly all private child support orders, then it would amount to little more than a government advance on the obligation. The government's role would amount to nothing more than making up for its own failure to adequately enforce private child support obligations.[16]

This argument has merit. Clearly, if the assured benefit is higher than the child support obligations of most nonresident parents, it becomes harder to distinguish it from a welfare program. However, there is nothing magical about the 90 percent figure. If the assured benefit level is such that 75 percent, rather than 90 percent, of nonresident parents' child support obligations exceed it, the integrity of the program is unlikely to be compromised. Indeed, the appropriate percentage is a matter of judgment. My own sense is that, as long as at least half the nonresident parents' obligations were higher than the assured benefit, the integrity of the assured benefit would not be compromised.

Lerman is critical of the high benefit levels and the income testing of benefits in both Wisconsin and New York, because they blur the distinction between the assured benefit and welfare. Furthermore, the two are related. High benefits increase costs, which, in turn, increase pressures to reduce costs through income testing. (Recall how quickly Wisconsin and New York strayed down the path of income testing.) Lerman argued that it is much better to have lower benefits and no income testing. He is right. My estimates show that a universal $2,000 assured benefit would reduce economic insecurity and welfare dependence more than the income-tested assured benefit of $3,000 that was to be tested in Wisconsin. This is because income testing the assured benefit reduces its value. To a resident parent with one child who earns $6,000, the assured benefit in Wisconsin is worth only $2,000, not $3,000. But a person needs to earn at least $6,000 to get off of welfare in Wisconsin. To a resident parent with $10,000 worth of earnings, the assured benefit is worth only $1,300.

LEAST HARMFUL LIMITATION OF COSTS

So far, this discussion has emphasized the dangers of making the assured benefit too high, because the experience in Wisconsin and New York suggests that strong pressures exist to combine a high benefit with steep income testing. Welfare colors everyone's thinking. Even as people strive to replace it, they are driven to re-create it.[17] That a low assured benefit with no income testing is better than a high benefit with income testing cannot be stressed enough, precisely because it runs so counter to the American welfare culture.

As the concept of an assured child support benefit moves closer to political enactment, methods of limiting its cost will be considered. Income testing the benefit is one. Lowering the assured benefit is another. The former is an undesirable compromise because it threatens the integrity of the system. The latter is less undesirable because it is more amenable to correction over time. Though social-insurance benefit levels were originally quite modest, they have been raised over time. In general, political scientists suggest that it is easier to start small.[18] Any assured child support benefit, therefore, even one as low as $500 per child per year, would be better than no assured child support benefit.

Having made the case against too high an assured benefit and for an initially low benefit, it is worth reiterating that, if the assured benefit is too low, it will do little to reduce economic insecurity and welfare dependence. Ultimately, how high the assured benefit should be is a matter of judgment, to be determined politically.

Another cost-saving alternative to reducing the value of the benefit is the German precedent of limiting eligibility for the assured benefit to three years. Other than limiting costs, the rationale for a time-limited benefit is that the first few years after divorce are likely to be the most traumatic. After three years, the argument goes, the divorced mother is more likely to have adjusted and to be on her feet again. However, private child support payments tend to erode over time. Thus, limiting the assured benefit to the first three years after a divorce or out-of-wedlock birth may have the effect of discontinuing the assurance when it is most needed. Moreover, providing an assured benefit for a short period of time and then withdrawing it lulls the custodial parent with a bit of security and then abruptly lets her down. For these reasons, if cost considerations and political circumstances require the acceptance of a lower than optimal assured benefit, it would be preferable to lower the benefit across the board rather than to limit it to a few years of eligibility.

APPENDIX 6.A/THE WELFARE CHILD SUPPORT SET-ASIDE VERSUS AN ASSURED CHILD SUPPORT BENEFIT

Although an assured child support benefit would promote the establishment of paternity, it is not the only way to do so. In fact, whereas only Wisconsin and New York are currently permitted to use the federal share of AFDC savings that result from increased child support enforcement to fund an assured benefit, all states are required by federal law to *set aside,* or ignore, the first $50 per month of child support paid in calculating the amount of the AFDC benefit. This $50 set-aside increases AFDC grants by up to $50 per month and, thereby, provides an incentive within the AFDC program to establish paternity. Why set up a new assured child support benefit when many of the same objectives can be accomplished within the AFDC system by the existing, or a more generous, child support set-aside?

There are some arguments for preferring a child support set-aside within welfare to an assured child support benefit. First, the set-aside, like the assured benefit, reduces economic insecurity. But it provides benefits more to those at the very bottom of the income distribution by limiting them to AFDC recipients. Second, like the assured benefit, a set-aside within welfare creates an incentive for custodial parents to cooperate in the establishment of paternity. But, whereas the assured benefit reduces the incentive for the nonresident parent to actually pay support, the set-aside is of benefit to the resident-parent family only to the extent that this parent actually pays support. Third, to the extent that young unwed mothers are likely to spend at least two or three years on welfare even if there were an assured benefit, an incentive within welfare is likely to be more effective in inducing cooperation to establish paternity than an assured benefit, because its effects would be felt by the resident parent so much sooner.

Each of these arguments is persuasive, but, as a whole, the case for an assured benefit is more so. Just as the better targeting of the child support set-aside within welfare is its strength, so too is it a critical source of weakness. Because it limits benefits to those on AFDC, the set-aside does nothing to reduce the economic insecurity of the millions of families with children eligible for child support who are not AFDC recipients.

Equally important, child support set-asides within welfare increase welfare benefits and, thereby, make welfare more attractive. In stark contrast, an assured child support benefit makes life outside welfare more attractive. Thus, whereas an assured child support benefit would decrease the extreme dependence endemic to AFDC, a child support set-aside would increase it. The difference is not trivial. A $2,000 assured child support benefit accompanied by an elimination of the $50 set-aside would reduce AFDC caseloads by 30 percent; an equally costly child support set-aside would increase caseloads by 13 percent.[19] Furthermore, the set-aside would shrink the poverty gap by only 12 percent, as opposed to 15 percent by the assured benefit.

There is one additional argument against creating incentives within welfare. Doing so distorts the philosophy and purposes of a welfare program. Welfare programs are designed to provide a minimally decent standard of living to those who cannot provide for themselves. They are programs of last resort. Traditionally, they make up the difference between whatever resources the family has and the minimum needed to survive. Providing incentives within the welfare system allows some families to continue receiving welfare even though their total incomes exceed the minimum.

Although these arguments establish a strong case for preferring an assured child support benefit to a child support set-aside within welfare, America's record of establishing paternity is still so abysmal that I now believe that, for the foreseeable future, the country needs both an assured child support benefit and a set-aside that lasts for three years. At this point, the United States cannot afford to dispense with any tool that will help to establish paternity.[20]

NOTES

1. In early 1986, Governor Mario Cuomo of New York appointed a panel of national experts to advise him on how to reduce poverty and welfare dependence. In December 1986, the panel issued the written report cited earlier ("New Social Contract") that recommended adoption of a new child support assurance system. Governor Cuomo proposed that the state adopt a percentage-of-income standard and routine income withholding immediately and test the assured child support benefit in a pilot program in eight counties. In 1987, the New York State legislature adopted neither a new child support standard nor routine income withholding, but it did approve the testing of an assured child support benefit that was steeply income tested and limited to welfare recipients. As of 1989, seven New York counties were testing the CAP. (By 1989, the New York legislature had adopted a modified

version of the Wisconsin percentage-of-income standard. Owing to the federal requirement of the Family Support Act of 1988, routine withholding will be adopted in the state by 1994.)

2. The description of the Swedish advance maintenance program is drawn from Garfinkel and Sorensen, "Sweden's Child Support System," pp. 509–515.

3. "Payment by the State of Advances on Child Maintenance," Recommendation No. R(82) 2, adopted by the Committee of Ministers of the Council of Europe on 4 February, 1982, and Explanatory Memorandum, Strasbourg, France: Council of Europe, 1982; Alfred J. Kahn and Sheila B. Kamerman, *Income Transfers for Families with Children: An Eight-Country Study*, Philadelphia: Temple University Press, chap. 6, 1983.

4. The maximum level of income at which the public subsidy is equal to zero can be calculated by dividing the assured benefit, or the maximum public subsidy, by the resident parent surtax. Both the assured benefit level and the surtax and, therefore, also the break-even level, depend upon the number of children owed support. Note that, if the nonresident parent pays anything, the break-even level of income for the resident parent is even lower.

5. For a detailed discussion of the regressivity of marginal tax rates arising from income testing, see E. Sadka, I. Garfinkel, and K. Moreland, "Income Testing and Social Welfare: An Optimal Tax-Transfer Model," pp. 291–313, and the comment by Kenneth Arrow in *Income-Tested Transfer Programs: The Case for and Against*, edited by Irwin Garfinkel, New York: Academic Press, 1982, pp. 319–323.

6. Although some economists have argued that income-tested benefits are more efficient than non-income-tested benefits in broader economic terms, what little evidence we have suggests that exactly the opposite is the case and that the differences are not very large either way (see Garfinkel, *Income-Tested Transfer Programs*).

7. The benefit reduction rate follows the proposed Wisconsin structure of 17 percent of income for one child, 25 percent for two children, 29 percent for three children, 31 percent for four children, and 34 percent for five or more children (for more detail, see Chapter 7).

8. As noted, the program is being tested in seven New York counties. In four of them, it is being made available to the entire AFDC caseload. In three others, CAP is available to only a randomly selected subset of the AFDC caseload. A randomly selected control group was also chosen, to facilitate evaluation of the program. The program began in Chautauqua and Ulster counties in October 1988, and it is now fully operational in all seven counties. As of July 1, 1991, there were 776 families enrolled in CAP. (See

Alan Werner and Nancy Burstein, "The New York State Child Assistance Program: Program Design, Operations and Early Impacts on Child Support Orders," paper presented at the Conference on Child Support and Child Well Being, Airlie House, Virginia, December, 1991, p. 18.)

9. Because the New York AFDC grant includes a shelter allowance that varies across counties, the state varied the assured benefit level across counties, to keep the relationship of the assured benefit to AFDC benefits constant.

10. The New York state CAP program, although not universal, is distinguished from, and more attractive than, welfare in several ways. Food stamps are paid in cash, offices are nicer, income reporting requirements are less onerous, and clients receive more personal casework services.

11. See Department of Health and Social Services, *Wisconsin Welfare Reform Study 1978*, Report and Recommendations of the Welfare Reform Study Advisory Committee, 1979.

12. Estimates are from the author's microsimulation of the intermediate run with an assured benefit of $2,000.

13. If taxing benefits does not limit costs sufficiently, limiting benefits to single-parent families is, for three reasons, a preferable temporary expedient to limiting benefits to low-income families. First, limiting benefits to single-parent families would not compromise the integrity of the program as severely as would income testing benefits. Second, the negative political effects of limiting benefits to single mothers are likely to be much smaller in the short than in the long run, because it takes time for the awareness that benefits are limited to single mothers to spread. Third, benefits limited to single parents would be easier to administer than benefits limited to low-income families. Eligibility determination is easier, and the amount of monitoring that must be done is less. Compared to limiting benefits to families with low income, however, confining benefits to single mothers does a poorer job of delivering benefits to those with greatest need, because, although limiting benefits to single parents implicitly targets those with greatest need, the targeting is implicit and imperfect. Despite this, on balance, limiting benefits to single parents is a preferable temporary expedient.

14. This is easy to see by considering the case of a resident-parent family with an income of $50,000 that receives a public subsidy of $500. Making the benefit taxable would recoup about 40 percent of the benefit, or about $200, leaving a public subsidy of about $300. Limiting benefits to families with incomes below, say, $40,000 would eliminate the entire $500 subsidy to them. Thus, although making benefits taxable can achieve considerable

savings without compromising the integrity of the assured benefit, the potential savings from imposing income limits are even
larger.

15. Microsimulation estimates of the author's in which the benefits
are income tested according to the Wisconsin formula.

16. Robert I. Lerman, "Child-Support Policies," in *Welfare Policy for
the 1990s*, edited by Phoebe H. Cottingham and David T.
Ellwood, Cambridge, Mass.: Harvard University Press, 1989,
pp. 219–246.

17. That even I fell prey to this lure indicates how strong it is, for I
have written extensively about the costs of income testing and,
from the start, conceived of the CSAS as a universal program.

18. For arguments about the wisdom of an incremental approach to
reform, see Aaron Wildavsky, *The Politics of the Budgetary Process*,
Boston: Little, Brown and Company, 1964; Richard P. Nathan,
"Food Stamps and Welfare Reform," *Policy Analysis*, Vol. 2, No. 1
(Winter 1976), pp. 61–70; Martha Derthick, *Policymaking for Social
Security*, Washington, D.C.: The Brookings Institution, 1979; W.
Andrew Achenbaum, *Social Security: Visions and Revisions*, Cam-
bridge, Mass.: Cambridge University Press, 1986.

19. Microsimulation estimates by the author.

20. In the past, I have advocated abolition of the $50 child support
set-aside (see testimony by Irwin Garfinkel at Hearings on the
Child Support Enforcement Program, Subcommittee on Public
Assistance and Unemployment Compensation, Committee on
Ways and Means, U.S. House of Representatives, March 2, 1988).

7 / Arguments Against the Child Support Assurance System

ARGUMENTS FOR AWARD STANDARDS

One of the criticisms of the CSAS is that legislated standards for child support awards are unfair, that each case should be considered on an individual basis. To these critics, I point out the realizations that led to federal adoption of legislated standards. As noted earlier, the 1980s marked an important institutional shift in American family law from individualized judicial determinations to the use of normative standards. In fact, the most visible example of this change is in the determination of the child support award. Traditionally, this award was set on a case-by-case basis by a judge in a hearing at which both parents had the opportunity to present evidence.[1]

The dramatic shift from judicial discretion to presumptive standards occurred when it became clear that the old system led to inequitable results. First, it resulted in awards that were much too low. The Census Bureau reports existing child support awards to resident mothers totaled nearly $10 billion in 1983. My colleagues and I estimated that, if either the percentage-of-income standard adopted by Wisconsin or the income-shares standard adopted by Colorado had been applied and updated in all cases that now have child support awards, the total owed would have been between $16.7 and $19.6 billion, or between 167 percent and 200 percent greater than existing awards.[2]

Judicial discretion also led to horizontal inequity in child support awards. Even within the same jurisdiction, supporting parents in similar circumstances were required to pay widely differing amounts.[3] When the number of broken marriages and out-of-wedlock births was small, greater equity was perhaps achieved by the old individualized system. In small communities, the judge knew the parents and the circumstances, so justice was better served by taking account of all particulars. But, as the number of cases grew and the system became impersonal, this method broke down. In practice, judges now do very little to tailor child support to particular circumstances.[4]

Another reason for dissatisfaction with the old system was the belief that it was inappropriate. The existence of public programs such as AFDC to assure a minimum income to children potentially eligible for child support means that the public has a direct financial stake in the amount of private child support paid by nonresident parents whose children could be recipients of public benefits. The lower the amount of support paid by nonresident parents, the greater the burden on taxpayers. How the support of poor children should be apportioned among the resident parent, the nonresident parent, and the public, therefore, is an issue more appropriate to the legislative than the judicial branch of government.

FATHERS' ABILITY TO PAY

Critics have suggested that perhaps the reason that a large proportion of nonresident parents pay no child support is not because of flaws in the system but simply because they cannot afford to pay. A lot of people used to believe this to be the case and some still do. Indeed, it is quite common to hear the phrase, "You can't get blood from a stone."

Table 7.1 presents estimates of the mean incomes of nonresident fathers by race and marital status of the resident mother. In 1983 the mean income for all nonresident fathers was $19,346. The

TABLE 7.1 / **Mean Income of Noncustodial Parents, in 1983 dollars**

Marital Status of Custodial Parents	Race of Custodial Parents		
	All	White	Nonwhite
Divorced	19,346	22,533	11,285
Never married	7,775	9,952	6,285
Separated	14,712	17,747	10,551
Divorced	23,600	24,760	17,824
Remarried	25,006	25,379	21,257

Source: Irwin Garfinkel and Donald Oellerich, "Noncustodial Fathers' Ability to Pay Child Support," *Demography*, Vol. 26, No. 2 (May 1989), Table 3, pp. 219–233.

average income of all prime-age men (that is, those 25–64 years old) was $22,482.[5] In other words, the average nonresident father's income was about 14 percent less than that of the average prime-age working man.

Differences in nonresident fathers' income by race and marital status (extrapolated from race and marital status of the mothers), however, were dramatic. The estimated incomes of nonwhite, nonresident fathers were only half those of their white counterparts. Even more dramatic were the differences within each race between the never-married and the divorced and remarried. Among whites, the average income of the latter was nearly three times that of the former, whereas among nonwhites the ratio was greater than 3 to 1.

These figures suggest that, although there are large variations in income, on the whole, nonresident parents are not particularly poor. Their average income is only somewhat less than the average for all prime-age men. Consequently, they can afford to pay reasonable amounts of child support.

The income figures in table 7.1 tell only part of the story. The amount of child support nonresident parents should pay depends not only on income but also on how much of their incomes nonresident fathers are expected to devote to child support. For example, if a nonresident parent's income is $19,000, his obligation would equal $1,900 if 10 percent were deemed the proportion of income a nonresident parent should share with his child. If 30 percent were deemed the appropriate sharing rate, however, his obligation would equal $5,700. Whether the nonresident parent can pay this amount of child support may depend upon whether he has started a new family or on some other normative judgment about how his income should be spent.

Does this mean that any estimate of the child support obligation is, ultimately, entirely subjective? Not quite, for it is possible to combine estimated incomes with a variety of judgments to derive a range of estimates of child support obligations that reflect both what the child should receive and how much the nonresident parent should be able to pay. A number of guidelines now in use provide formulas to derive what are considered to be equitable child support amounts. The guidelines differ in the factors they take into account in determining how much a nonresident father should be able to pay.

Most states have now adopted guidelines similar to either the income-shares guideline developed by the OCSE and implemented first in Colorado or the percentage-of-income guideline developed in Wisconsin. As noted, under the latter, the child support obligation depends only upon the income of the nonresident parent and the number of children owed support. Under the Colorado guideline, the obligation also depends upon the income of the resident parent and the child care and medical care expenditures of the resident parent for the children eligible for support. Under yet another guideline, developed by Judge Melson in Delaware, the obligation depends upon whether or not the nonresident parent has started a new family, and poor nonresident parents are excused from any obligation.

The advantages and disadvantages of the various guidelines and the principles upon which they are based were discussed at length in chapter 5. The point to be made here is that, whatever guideline is used, nonresident parents can pay a great deal more child support than they now do. Comparison of the amount that would have been owed under the three guidelines with the amount actually owed and paid in 1983 reveals that the difference between what was owed ($9.7 billion) and what was paid ($6.8 billion) was dwarfed by the difference between these numbers and the estimates derived from the guidelines. Nonresident fathers can pay from $24 billion to $30 billion or, at the least, about two and a half times the legal obligations under the old system and more than three times the amount they have been actually paying. These estimates strongly suggest that the poor performance of the private child support system in recent years is not attributable to an inability of nonresident parents to pay but rather to a system that allowed a large portion of nonresident parents to avoid responsibility for their children.

POOR NONRESIDENT FATHERS

Saying that fathers as a whole can afford to pay more child support still leaves open the question of what to do about those fathers who are poor. If a father is excused from contributing, he gets the message that he has nothing of value to share with his child. If he is required to contribute, he gets the message that, no matter how little he has, he still has something worthwhile to offer his child. The requirement of some sharing, therefore, treats the father with greater respect and gets more resources to the child.

Furthermore, fathers who live with their children are expected to share whatever little they have with them. Indeed, if they fail to share with their children when they live with them, resident fathers are guilty of child neglect, if not child abuse. In such cases the state has the legal right to take their children away from them. Why, then, should fathers who live apart from their children be entirely excused from any obligation to share with them?

My position on this issue became clear to me during a meeting with Secretary Reivitz of Wisconsin's DHSS. I met with her soon after she had started her new position in 1982 to explain the CSAS and to delineate where Wisconsin stood on implementation of the plan. She was skeptical about making poor fathers pay. I was insistent that they pay something. We went back and forth on this until finally she asked, "Even if they're in *prison*?" I paused for just a moment. "Yes, they get paid in prison." I left her office, sure I had lost her and that she thought I was a fanatic on the point. But I continue to believe that expecting all fathers to contribute to their children's support is the most humane policy.

Although I am adamant that poor fathers should pay something, how much they should pay is an issue I still struggle with.

Should poor nonresident fathers pay a smaller percentage of child support? Although both the income-shares standard and the Wisconsin percentage-of-income standard superficially appear to be in agreement that even poor nonresident parents must pay some child support, they differ in that the income-shares standard explicitly provides more favorable treatment to poor nonresident parents than the Wisconsin standard, which enables judges to depart from the standard if the nonresident parent is poor. Some child support standards, including the well-known Delaware standard, do specifically exempt poor nonresident parents from paying anything.[6]

To grant that poor nonresident parents should share at least some of their income with their children does not imply that the sharing rate should be the same as for more well-to-do parents. Whether the sharing rates for poor nonresident parents should be lower is a complex question, with a strong case for it and a strong, but less well understood, case against it.

The case for a lower child support sharing rate is the same as the case for a progressive, income tax. The poor are less able to pay. Whereas 17 percent of income is a substantial burden for a middle-income nonresident father, for a poor nonresident father, it may be truly oppressive.

The case against a lower child support sharing rate is twofold. First, a good starting point for determining how much nonresident parents should share with their children is the amount they would be sharing if they were living together. To achieve equity, the share of income devoted to the child should be similar for resident and nonresident parent. In addition, if the share paid by nonresident parents is much lower, an undesirable economic incentive is created to live apart from the child. No research suggests that, among fathers who reside with their children, the poor spend a smaller proportion of their income on the children than middle-income fathers. Indeed, the evidence suggests either that the proportions are about the same or that the poor actually spend a slightly higher percentage.

The second argument against a lower sharing rate is that it must result in lower child support payments to resident parents and their children or higher taxes to supplement it, or an increase in the sharing rate of nonpoor nonresident parents. None of these is particularly desirable. Resident parents and their children are worse off financially than nonresident parents. Taxpayers already feel overburdened and seem unwilling to pay sufficient taxes to finance existing government services. Resident parents and taxpayers could be spared to some extent by increasing the sharing rate of nonpoor nonresident parents, in order to hold constant their total child support obligation. This results in a progressive rate structure in which a greater percentage of income is required for child support as the nonresident parent's income goes up.

A simple example illustrates how this can be done. Consider the Wisconsin percentage-of-income standard, which calls for child support awards of 17 percent of income for one child. Now suppose it is deemed desirable to reduce the amount to 10 percent of income for the first $5,000 of earnings. The effect of this reduction on the nonresident parent with an income of $15,000 is as follows: Without the reduction, the child support obligation is equal to $2,550. With the reduction, the child support obligation is equal to 10 percent of $5,000 plus 17 percent of $10,000, for a total of only $2,200. To bring the obligation up to $2,550, the rate on this nonresident parent's income in excess of $5,000 must be increased to 20.5 percent.

I have always advocated a proportional, rather than a progressive, rate structure for several reasons. It is simple, it has intuitive equity appeal, and it is more progressive than the existing rate structure, which is regressive. All of these arguments still hold. Yet I am increasingly sympathetic to a lower rate for the poor nonresident parent. In part, this is a reaction to the fact that no one is taking my advice on this matter. The Wisconsin legislature accepted my recommendation for a proportional rate structure but then created a loophole for judges to depart from the standard if the nonresident parent was poor. The standard proposed by the Cuomo administration in New York and passed by the New York legislature treats the child support obligation of a poor nonresident parent as a debt to be repaid when income is higher. The income-shares standard developed for the OCSE, which is regressive on the whole, has much lower rates for below-poverty-level incomes. And finally, in early 1990, when I was asked to provide advice to the British government on child support reform I met with Prime Minister Thatcher's Secretary of State for Social Security, Tony Newton. Over lunch he and his principal assistant made it clear that they thought I was a bit too tough on poor men. Finding myself to the right of the Thatcher government was, and remains, extremely disconcerting.

Circumstances have also changed. The Tax Reform Act of 1986 lowered marginal tax rates of the personal income tax in the United States to below what they were in the early 1980s. Thus, the adverse effects on work effort of having a progressive rate structure in the child support system should be smaller now. I still adamantly believe that poor fathers should pay something; I am open, however, to the position that the percentage they pay should be less than nonpoor fathers.

EFFECTS OF STRONGER CHILD SUPPORT ENFORCEMENT ON MOTHERS AND CHILDREN

Some argue that stronger enforcement of child support will induce angry men to retaliate against the mothers of their children. Indeed, in the early 1980s, when I first started speaking publicly about the inadequacies of the old child support system and the promise of a new child support assurance system, one professor warned me that I would "have the blood of women on my hands." A more general version of the same argument is that the men who are not paying child support are obviously not model fathers; yet they would get more involved with the children and their mothers if compelled to pay support, and their influence on the children would be negative. According to this view, the so-called inadequacies of the old child support system represented a desirable accommodation to the unpleasant realities of life and should not be tampered with.

This argument may be reinforced by recent census data indicating, as mentioned, that four out of ten women with children potentially eligible for child support who do not have a child support award report that the reason they do not is because they do not want one.[7] Do these figures suggest that the alleged shortcomings of the old system simply reflect the good sense of mothers trying to avoid contact with fathers that might be bad for the children? The answer must be, in part, yes.

There are some fathers who are a dangerous threat to their

children and the mothers of their children. Forgoing child support in order to make a clean break with such fathers may be in the mother's, the child's, and society's best interest. But cases in which the nonresident father poses a serious threat to his children or former mate, while memorable and to be taken seriously, are hardly typical. Most nonresident fathers are not dangerous. It is unclear whether a policy of abrogating the child support responsibility of fathers who pose a physical threat to children or their mothers is the best way to protect them. If it becomes known that violence or the threat of violence leads to the cancellation of the child support responsibility, this might actually promote such behavior and be counterproductive.

Still, although not a physical threat to their children, it is possible that most nonresident fathers who are paying too little or no support would be a bad influence on their children if they became more involved in their lives. Exactly the opposite, however, is also possible. It may be that, if these fathers became more involved in the lives of their children as a result of being compelled to pay child support, their children would benefit not only from the extra money but also from the extra attention. At this point, there is no conclusive evidence on the matter. We don't even know the extent to which stronger enforcement of child support would lead to greater involvement of nonresident fathers. My belief is that stronger enforcement would lead to somewhat greater involvement, which, on net, would be positive for the children.[8]

Even if all of the mothers who did not want awards were acting in the best interests of their children and the larger society, that still leaves over half of the mothers without child support awards who wanted one. (See chapter 4 for discussion of the potential conflict of interest between resident mothers and their children and the rest of society.) Moreover, some of the mothers who did not want child support awards under the old system would have wanted them if the system had worked better and the benefits of having an award had been higher. It is difficult to attribute the low level of awards and the widespread nonpayment of those awards to the poor motivation of the mothers. At most, only a small portion of the shortcomings of the old child support system can be dismissed as reflecting lack of interest on the part of the mothers.

WITHHOLDING AS GOVERNMENTAL INTERFERENCE

The primary justification for routine income withholding of child support payments from wages and other forms of income is that it will increase the amount and regularity of payments and reduce economic insecurity. Tom Corbett, with whom I worked on development of the CSAS, has also likened child support to a preeminent debt. This debt should be paid as certainly as taxes are paid. Routine withholding assures that income and payroll taxes are paid, and it would do the same for child support obligations.

There are two major objections to routine income withholding of child support obligations. It substantially increases costs and imposes "big brother" style governmental interference in private family matters. It imposes administrative costs on employers and government. As it turns out, however, the burden on employers is not so great. They are already withholding social security and income taxes from wages. Many, if not most, already withhold for more individualized purposes like private retirement benefits, and most, including small businesses, have computerized their payroll records. Finally, in Wisconsin when routine income withholding was enacted, a large proportion of employers were already withholding child support because their employees had become delinquent in their payments. For all of these reasons, Wisconsin employers did not object to legislation that mandated routine income withholding. For similar reasons, four years later employers' groups in America as a whole did not oppose the routine income withholding provisions of the Family Support Act.

The administrative costs to the seven state governments that already receive and disburse child support payments made on behalf of all the children in the state are negligible. In the other states that receive payments nearly exclusively for children on welfare, the number of cases handled by child support offices would increase substantially. Costs for staff, envelopes, and stamps would increase. The extra administrative costs would not be trivial. It is difficult to say, however, how large these extra costs would be, because the extent to which they would be offset by other administrative savings from not having to pursue delinquent payments is unknown. On balance, the administrative burdens imposed by routine income withholding are likely to be quite modest. Thus, the cost argument is not very persuasive.

Opponents of routine income withholding have also character-ized it as big brother, big government interference in private fam-ily matters. Some fathers' groups ask why government should interfere in the majority of cases where support is being paid? The response is quite simple. Private child support is not a private family matter when the family has broken apart or never formed. No state or country treats child support as if it were a strictly private family matter.

Unfortunately, it is not true that child support is paid on time in a majority of the cases. It is true that, during the course of any year, about half the nonresident fathers pay all of the child sup-port they owe. But many of those who pay all they owe one year, pay less than they owe the next, and many more are delinquent in their payments during the course of the year. Recall that 70 percent of the nonresident parents in Wisconsin became at least two months delinquent in their child support payments within three years. Surely it is better and less interfering to routinely withhold child support in all cases than to withhold only in re-sponse to delinquency and, thereby, brand over 70 percent of nonresident parents as lawbreakers.

The truth of the matter is that routine withholding of child support is a useful government service to nonresident parents who truly wish to pay child support. I have two children in col-lege. At the end of each month, I send them a check to cover their living expenses. On occasion I forget and they call and gently remind me. Neither they nor I think that my forgetfulness is a manifestation of some underlying hostility. But all divorced men can appreciate that neither their former wives, nor even they, would be so quick to dismiss the possibility that forgetting to pay child support was an indication of underlying hostility on their part. Divorce is tough enough under the best of circumstances. For those who plan to pay, eliminating any potential source of conflict is a blessing; so it is better to have the support withheld and not have to worry about it.

ARGUMENTS AGAINST AN ASSURED BENEFIT

Because America has already made so much progress toward the CSAS on the collection side, most arguments against it are now directed at the benefit. These arguments focus on the expanding role of government, the cost, the inadequate targeting, and the adverse incentives.

The Expanding Role of Government

The assured benefit is opposed by some because they believe it will expand the role of government. Limited government is certainly closely connected to civil liberties and freedom.[9] Even the former Communist countries now appreciate the connection among limited government, capitalism, and economic growth and development. So, although an increase in the role of government should not be undertaken lightly, especially in a country that justifiably takes pride in its tradition of limited government, in the case of the assured child support benefit, the increase in government's role is quite small and could even be negative.

If anything, it is the collection components of the child support assurance system that involve the largest increase in government. Establishment of paternity, setting of child support awards by a numerical standard, universal immediate withholding of child support, and universal payments to a government agency, all involve substantial government interference in the private affairs of citizens. Furthermore, as noted, the collection-side reforms necessitated a sizable bureaucracy. As a consequence of the 1984 and 1988 federal child support enforcement legislation, all child support payments will be made to, and then distributed by, government agencies. Enactment of an assured benefit merely changes the amount of the checks that these agencies will be mailing to resident parents and adds a bit of extra bookkeeping.

Indeed, it is likely that the net effect of an assured benefit would be to reduce the size of government and administrative costs. Although the assured benefit would increase the total number of families receiving government subsidies, it would decrease the number receiving AFDC and other welfare benefits. Welfare programs are costly to administer and interfere a great deal in the lives of their beneficiaries. In contrast, the assured benefit would be very cheap to administer and would involve practically no extra interference in the lives of its beneficiaries. If the assured benefit reduces welfare dependence substantially, therefore, despite the fact that it increases the total number of beneficiaries, it is likely to reduce administrative costs and the overall scope of government.

Cost

The major argument I hear against an assured benefit is cost. Although the estimates in chapter 3 suggest that, in the long run, even a very generous child support assurance system can be cost-neutral, that does not imply that the assured benefit is costless. The CSAS as a whole is estimated to be cost-neutral because the increased costs of the assured benefit are offset by AFDC savings that arise principally from increased child support payments and secondarily from its improved work incentives. The AFDC savings that result from improved child support enforcement could be devoted to a host of other uses such as child care or deficit reduction. Even if the CSAS as a whole is cost-neutral, therefore, the assured benefit component can be considered independent of the collection provisions, and it clearly has a cost.

Couldn't the CSAS actually save money if the government didn't have to pay for an assured benefit? Clearly, the answer is yes. Although it is possible that the assured benefit would reduce total administrative costs, it would definitely increase total transfer costs. But, obviously, because something has a cost doesn't mean it is not worth doing. As economists are fond of saying, "There is no free lunch." To determine whether AFDC savings that result from improved child support collections should be devoted to uses other than an assured benefit, two questions need to be answered. The first is, How large are the costs of an assured benefit? The second, and more important, question is, Do the benefits exceed the costs?

Table 3.1, which analyzed costs and benefits for the CSAS as a whole, can be used to calculate for the assured benefit alone the costs to government and the benefits in reduced welfare dependence and poverty. Each row of the table presents two benefits, reductions in poverty and AFDC caseloads, and net costs to the government treasury of the CSAS at various levels of an assured child support benefit, ranging from none to $3,000. If we assume that the assured benefit has no effect on paternity establishment, a very conservative assumption, the benefits and costs of the assured benefit alone can be seen by subtracting the positive assured benefit row from the row with no assured benefit. Thus, under the modest-improvement scenario, by subtracting the second from the first row in Table 3.1 we see that the net cost of an assured benefit of $1,000 is only $200 million. Moreover, the cost is similar in the short and intermediate runs. So, on the scale of the national budget, the net costs of a $1,000 assured child support benefit are trivial. Unfortunately, the measured benefits are equally modest. The poverty gap is reduced by only 1 percent and AFDC caseloads are reduced by 2 percent or 3 percent.

The net costs of a $2,000 assured child support benefit range between $1 and $2 billion. The benefits are also commensurably larger. In the short run, an assured benefit of $2,000 would reduce the poverty gap by 5 percent, instead of by 2 percent or 3 percent, and AFDC caseloads by 8 percent, rather than 3 percent or 4 percent. In the intermediate run, the reduction in the poverty gap is quite substantial: 17 percent. This is 5 percentage points higher than that achieved by improvements in private child support alone. AFDC caseload reductions are equally substantial: 20 percent. In this case, however, more than half of the reduction is due to the assured benefit. Furthermore, this estimate of the importance of an assured benefit is too low because it assumes that paternity establishment is not affected by the presence or amount of an assured child support benefit.

Only the assured benefit of $3,000 can be said to be very costly, and even it is equal to only $2.8 to $3.2 billion. But the benefits of a $3,000 assured benefit are truly striking. Even in the short run, the assured benefit increases the reduction in the poverty gap from a mere 2 percent to a respectable 9 percent. Similarly, caseload reductions go from a negligible 2 percent to a very noticeable 14 percent. By the intermediate run, a $3,000 assured child support benefit reduces the poverty gap and AFDC caseloads by nearly a quarter and a third! These rates are twice and more than triple those achieved solely by improved child support collections. I have no hesitation in concluding that the benefits outweigh the costs at all levels of an assured child support benefit.

Inadequate Targeting

The third argument against an assured benefit is that it provides benefits to families with incomes substantially above the poverty level. In general, programs that provide benefits to the nonneedy should be scrutinized with great care. In view of the large federal deficit, it would seem more important than ever to target public expenditures to the truly needy.

But we have just seen that, despite its lack of explicit targeting by income, in practice the assured benefit turns out to be quite effectively aimed at the right segment. Recall, for example, that, in the intermediate run, a $2,000 assured benefit costs only $1 billion, yet achieves an additional 3-percentage-point reduction in the poverty gap.

An assured child support benefit concentrates its benefits on the poor recipients naturally by virtue of assortative mating. Like tend to mate with like. Those who are highly educated tend to mate with other highly educated individuals and vice versa. Thus, nonresident parents with incomes low enough to require government subsidy to bring their payments up to the assured benefit level are likely to be making payments to a relatively poor resident-parent family. Making the public-subsidy portion of the assured benefit taxable for income tax purposes further increases the effective targeting of the benefits without requiring a separate welfarelike test of means. Families with incomes in excess of the median for families with children—$25,705 in 1985—receive only 20 percent of the total public subsidy.

Furthermore, the costs of trying to confine the benefits to only the very needy are high. One has only to look at the current welfare system to recognize the problems inherent in too much targeting. To confine benefits to only the very needy, AFDC substantially reduces benefits as income increases. For single mothers who can earn very little or who marry men who can earn very little, this creates serious disincentives to work and remarry. That is acceptable if the program is to provide only temporary aid. But recall, there is need for a program that provides ongoing income supplementation, for which welfare is unsuitable precisely because it is so targeted. In contrast, an assured child support benefit is admirably suited to income supplementation precisely because it doesn't attempt to target benefits to only the poor.

Adverse Incentives

A fourth argument against an assured benefit is that it would reduce the incentive for low-income, nonresident fathers to pay child support. If the father's child support obligation is less than the assured benefit, his payments serve only to offset the costs of the assured benefit and are of no help to his children. Similarly, although the mothers of these children have an incentive to secure a child support award, once they have one, they have no motivation to pursue the fathers to persuade them to make payments. The larger the assured benefit, the greater the number of parents with no private reward for payment of child support.

At first, this seems like a serious drawback. Theoretically, it is even possible that this disincentive would lead to a larger decrease in payments than the increase in payments created by the incentive to establish paternity. In practice, this seems very unlikely. In the case of establishing paternity, the incentive of the assured benefit is reinforced by the law. In the case of payments, the incentive and the law work in opposite directions. The assured benefit removes the incentive of child support payments benefiting the child. But nonresident parents are still required to pay child support. The situation in this case becomes very analogous to paying taxes. Citizens derive very little *direct* benefit from paying taxes, but they are liable to stiff penalties if they fail to pay. As child support enforcement becomes increasingly strong, it will increasingly resemble the tax system. Yet, even though an improved child support enforcement system is likely to overwhelm this disincentive effect, the disincentive provides a reason for not making the assured benefit too large, for, the larger it is, the greater the proportion of the population who receive no reward for paying child support.

Finally, the assured benefit creates an incentive for low-income parents to live apart or at least claim to live apart. So long as the child support paid by the nonresident parent is equal to that received by the resident parent, child support creates no financial advantages to failing to marry or to separating. But for some families the assured benefit makes the payment received by the resident parent larger than the payment made by the nonresident parent. The larger the assured benefit level and the greater the difference between payments made and payments received, the greater the financial advantage to the couple to separate or feign separation.

Of course, AFDC already provides such adverse incentives.

Empirical research suggests that the effects of these adverse incentives are small.[10] But the assured benefit would be less stigmatizing than AFDC and would extend the disincentives to a broader population group. These adverse incentives are a regrettable, but unavoidable, cost of an assured child support benefit. That the incentive to live apart increases and the incentive to pay child support decreases as the assured benefit increases is another argument, in addition to costs, for not having too high an assured benefit.

Despite the fact that some of the arguments against an assured child support benefit have some merit, the overall case for it remains strong.

NOTES

1. Historically, statutes authorized courts to set child support at their discretion, with only very general guidelines such as an amount "deemed just and reasonable." In the 1970s, concern about the need for more determinative standards arose, and a proliferation of legislative and administrative guidelines set forth laundry lists of factors to be considered by the court in establishing the amount of a support award (see, for example, Doris Freed and Timothy Walker, "Family Law in the Fifty States: An Overview," *Family Law Quarterly*, Vol. 20, 1987, pp. 439 and 550–551).
2. Oellerich, Garfinkel, and Robins, "Private Child Support, Table 2, pp. 3–24. For evidence of public backing for higher child support standards, see Tom Corbett, Irwin Garfinkel, and Nora Cate Schaeffer, "Public Opinion about a Child Support Assurance System," *Social Service Review*, Vol. 62, No. 4 (December 1988), pp. 632–648.
3. The two most frequently cited empirical studies on this point are White and Stone, "Study of Alimony and Child Support Rulings," pp. 75–91; Yee, "What Really Happens in Child Support Cases," pp. 21–70.
4. Marygold S. Melli, Howard S. Erlanger, and Elizabeth Chambliss, "The Process of Negotiation: An Exploratory Investigation in the Context of No-Fault Divorce," *Rutgers Law Review*, Vol. 40, No. 3, 1988, pp. 1133–1172.
5. U.S. Bureau of the Census, *Money Income of Households, Families, and Persons in the United States: 1983*, Current Population Reports, Consumer Income Series P-60, No. 146, Washington, D.C.: U.S. Government Printing Office, 1985.

6. See Family Court of the State of Delaware, *The Delaware Child Support Formula: Study and Evaluation,* Report to the 132nd General Assembly, April 1984, or *The Delaware Child Support (Melson) Formula* (revised 1984); the Family Court of the State of Delaware, "Procedure in Deciding Child Support Cases (1984)," in *Improving Child Support Practice,* Vol. 1, Washington, D.C.: American Bar Association, pp. 169–174, 1986.

7. U.S. Bureau of the Census, "Child Support and Alimony: 1985," Table 2. I subtracted from the total without awards those who had agreements pending or property settlements in lieu of support.

8. For a fuller discussion of these issues and a preliminary research design, see Irwin Garfinkel and Sara McLanahan, "The Effects of the Child Support Provisions of the Family Support Act of 1988 on Child Well-Being," *Population Research and Policy Review,* September, 1990, pp. 205–234.

9. For the classic statement, see John Stuart Mill, *On Liberty,* London: Longman, 1864. For a more recent statement, see Milton Friedman, *Capitalism and Freedom.* Chicago: University of Chicago Press, 1982.

10. Garfinkel and McLanahan, *Single Mothers,* pp. 55–63.

8 / Summary and Conclusion

THE CASE FOR A FULL-FLEDGED CSAS

Although the nation is in the process of adopting a child support assurance system, it has not completed the task. Despite the adoption of guidelines, the courts are still heavily involved in determining the child support obligation. Only a few states have implemented universal, routine withholding. All of the states are a long way from universal establishment of paternity. And, perhaps most important, neither the federal government nor any state has adopted an assured child support benefit.

Such a benefit will simultaneously reduce economic insecurity and welfare dependence. Private child support is irregular. An assured benefit provides a secure base of child support, which is of value to single mothers from all income classes but particularly to those with low earning capacity. For them, this secure base makes life outside welfare far more tolerable.

If the economic security of single mothers and their children is of no concern, it is easy to reduce welfare rolls. Just cut benefits. That's what we've been doing since 1975, and the percentage of

single mothers collecting welfare has dropped from about 60 percent to 40 percent. Conversely, if welfare dependence is of no
concern, it's easy to increase economic security. Just make welfare
benefits more generous. That is exactly what was done between
1955 and 1975, and, not surprisingly, the proportion of single
mothers dependent on welfare went from less than 40 percent to
about 60 percent.[1] What the nation needs now are policies that
reduce both insecurity and dependence. That is why an assured
benefit is so attractive.

An assured benefit would also promote child support collections.[2] First, it would promote the establishment of paternity. It
gives mothers who want to make a life outside of welfare a con-
crete reason for determining paternity. By the same token, it gives
welfare officials and community activists a tool in their efforts to
reduce both welfare caseloads and economic insecurity.

Second, an assured child support benefit would help focus attention on the role of fathers in providing child support. It gives
explicit recognition to the fact that single mothers cannot be expected to support their children fully. The next obvious question
is, Who should pay for this assurance, the public or nonresident
fathers? Some on the Left would say that the government should
pay the entire amount, and some on the Right would say that
the government should pay nothing. The logical compromise is a
partnership in which most of the support is paid for by nonresident fathers. Deciding the exact terms of the partnership would
necessitate a public process that would inevitably call attention to
the role of fathers. In the near future, this would almost certainly
result in reinforcing efforts at child support collection.

Third, a federal assured benefit could be used to give the federal
government jurisdiction in enforcing child support obligations
and, thereby, strengthen interstate child support enforcement.

Of course, it is possible for the nation to adopt an assured child
support benefit, as well as child support guidelines and routine
income withholding, in a piecemeal fashion that neither provides
a federal assured benefit nor completes the shift from a judicial to
an administrative system of support enforcement. A full-fledged
federal CSAS administered by the Social Security Administration
would complete this shift. A few states have nearly completed
this type of shift, and they are the ones that are the most effective

at collecting support. A federal CSAS would also facilitate child support enforcement for the large proportion of cases that cross state lines.

The General Lesson: The CSAS as a Universal Program

To promote self-reliance and, at the same time, reduce the economic insecurity of families headed by single mothers, I have argued that the nation should rely more heavily on a universal program, a new child support assurance system that provides benefits to these families whatever their incomes and, thereby, reduces reliance on welfare programs, which aid only the poor. In general, a more universal approach is the way to simultaneously reduce insecurity and dependence.

A child support assurance system promotes work among single mothers who are poor and would otherwise be dependent on welfare, because it provides a source of income other than welfare, which is not reduced as earnings increase, as welfare is. All universal benefits have this property and, therefore, provide the greatest incentive for the poor to work. For example, one recent study estimated that, if welfare recipients could obtain health care coverage as good as Medicaid when they were employed, the employment rate of mothers on welfare would increase by about 25 percent, and welfare caseloads would drop by a corresponding percentage.[3]

A child support assurance system reduces economic insecurity via the same mechanism: a source of income outside welfare. Like all universal programs, it provides assistance, not just to those who have fallen into poverty, but to all those who share the same predicament, be it unemployment or the absence of a parent. And, like America's social insurance programs, the child support benefits are related to previous living standards.

The CSAS, and universal programs in general, also promote equality of opportunity. Programs like AFDC, that aid only those with low incomes, must reduce benefits as the income of beneficiaries increases. In so doing, these welfare programs impose tax (benefit reduction) rates that are higher than those required to finance the programs. This is equivalent to imposing regressive tax rates in the overall tax-transfer system. Whereas the rich lose part of what they earn through taxes, the poor lose an even bigger part of what they earn through benefit reductions.

Precisely because welfare programs lead to this regressivity, they are not a desirable way of supplementing the incomes of the poor who are expected to work. Poor mothers can earn less in the market than nonpoor. The highly regressive tax rates that arise out of AFDC, food stamps, and Medicaid exacerbate this inequality; they stack the deck against the poor mother who tries to achieve through hard work. Is it any wonder that the poorest half of single mothers works so much less than the half with greater earning abilities? Furthermore, owing to their higher tax rates, welfare programs create greater incentives for the poor to work at intermittent, informal, and illegal jobs, from which the earnings need not be reported. This is surely a violation of equality of opportunity.

Finally, a child support assurance system would integrate beneficiaries into the social mainstream. AFDC and other welfare programs segregate the poor by placing them in separate programs administered by special bureaucracies. In the CSAS, as in all universal programs, one bureaucracy deals with rich and poor alike. Free public education has been one of the principal integrative social institutions in America. It is difficult to imagine that the United States would have had so much social mobility if the public had paid for only the education of poor children.

As good as universal programs are, they have drawbacks. The greater the number of people who receive benefits, the more costly the program to nonbeneficiaries. Programs that provide benefits to everyone, such as public education, are more costly to upper-middle-income and upper-income people than programs that provide similar benefits only to the poor. Thus, because universal programs cost them more than welfare programs, the narrow self-interest of citizens with above-average incomes leads them to favor means-tested programs. Only if a universal program offers substantial advantages to people with above-average incomes are the extra costs worth it to them.

The more pervasive a problem, the greater the case for resolving it with a universal program. When the problem affects the middle- and upper-middle-income groups, they may have more to gain from a universal, than a welfare, program. Poverty is the most extreme manifestation of economic insecurity. But insecurity is not confined to the poor. Unemployment, for example, is most severe for the poor, but it is often severe even for middle-income and upper-middle-income Americans. The fact that Unemployment Insurance provides benefits to all Americans, rather than to only the poorest, reflects the pervasiveness of the problem of unemployment and society's commitment to reducing the economic insecurity of the unemployed population regardless of their degree of poverty. That is why the United States and all other Western industrialized nations have unemployment insurance programs. Similar arguments exist for old-age insurance and survivors insurance.

Are the economic insecurity and poverty of mother-only families pervasive social problems, or are they confined to a small segment of our poorest citizens? The evidence clearly indicates that they are pervasive. Nearly half of the children who live in mother-only families are poor. Most of the others have suffered large drops in income but do not qualify for welfare benefits. It is hard to avoid the conclusion that welfare is no substitute for a program that provides support to the children of all single mothers.

Despite the fact that women obviously have a disproportionate interest in how such families are treated, this is not just a women's issue. Nearly one of every two fathers who has a daughter today can expect her to head her own family. Similarly, one of the two fathers can expect his child to live in a mother-only family before growing up and leaving home. And nearly one of every two men in the next generation will grow up in such a family. Because any of us could be affected, it may be in the best interest of people of all incomes to provide some benefits and services to all mother-only families. If a man's daughter, for instance, runs the risk of divorce but not of poverty, it may be cheaper for him to pay more taxes for an efficient, universal, child support collection system than to pay less taxes for a system that serves the poor alone. For, in the latter case, he may be forced to provide the only support his daughter and her children will receive (with the children's father not contributing a cent). And, finally, it is surely in the long-term self-interest of Americans, whatever their income, race, or ethnic group, to increase the economic security and self-reliance of single-parent families, in which so many of the nation's children will live. This is especially true if security and self-reliance can be obtained without encouraging, indeed even discouraging, the formation of single-parent families.

Two lessons emerge from this detailed examination of the child support system. First, a child support assurance system would simultaneously reduce economic insecurity, poverty, and welfare dependence. Second, the CSAS can simultaneously promote security and independence because of its universality.

The Bottom Line: What It Will Cost

As for the policymakers' concerns about cost, chapter 3 pointed out that, in the short run, a national CSAS with a $2,000 assured benefit for the first child would reduce the poverty gap by 5 percent and AFDC caseloads by 8 percent. In the short run, the costs of such a program would be only about $1 billion a year. As improvements in paternity establishment and other child support enforcement practices lead to increases in eligibility for the assured benefit and increases in collections, economic insecurity and welfare dependence will fall along with costs. Indeed, our intermediate-run estimates for a $2,000 assured benefit for the first child are that the poverty gap and welfare caseloads would each decrease by about one-fifth, at a cost to the Treasury of only $100 million.

These estimates suggest that a new child support assurance system represents a marked improvement over the old one. Thus, it is not surprising that the country is in the process of abandoning the old and moving toward the new system.

The estimates also highlight the limitations of a child support assurance system in reducing economic insecurity and welfare dependence. Although definitely noteworthy and worth achieving, a one-fifth reduction in poverty and welfare dependence still leaves 80 percent of both problems. Even if, in the long run, the private child support system worked to perfection, 60 percent of the poverty gap and over half of the AFDC caseload would remain. The CSAS can achieve a great deal, but much more remains to be done. Other policies that simultaneously reduce insecurity and welfare dependence are needed to complement child support assurance.[4]

NOTES

1. Robert Moffitt, "Incentive Effects of the U.S. Welfare System: A Review," Institute for Research on Poverty Special Report Series #48, Madison, Wis.: University of Wisconsin-Madison, 1990. According to Moffitt, AFDC Participation rates of female-headed households with children were 36 percent in 1967, 62 percent in 1975, and, 42 percent in 1987.
2. The assured benefit could also reduce child support payments by decreasing the incentive for fathers to pay amounts below the assured benefit level. As discussed in chapter 7, however, this effect is likely to be swamped by the effects discussed later in this chapter.
3. R. Moffitt and B. L. Wolfe, "The Effect of the Medicaid Program on Welfare Participation and Labor Supply," Institute for Research on Poverty Discussion Paper #909-90, Madison, Wis.: University of Wisconsin-Madison, 1990.
4. For a discussion of some such policies see Garfinkel and McLanahan, *Single Mothers;* David Ellwood, *Poor Support: Poverty in the American Family,* Basic Books, 1988; Sheila B. Kamerman and Alfred J. Kahn, *Mothers Alone: Strategies for a Time of Change,* Dover, Mass.: Auburn House Publishing Company, 1988.

Index